THE
PIVOT

PRAISE FOR *THE PIVOT*

Becky Leach is a gifted, beautiful writer. Her words captivate you and make you feel like you're having a conversation with her, sitting cross-legged on her living room floor, enjoying a cup of coffee. She's real and thoughtful as she recounts her story of abuse. But she doesn't leave it there. In *The Pivot*, she shares how she has wrestled with God to know Him more, trust Him more and how she began a journey of glorious restoration as only God can do. We have a choice when things don't turn out like we think they should. She chose to pivot and God is using her to tell His story.

LISA CLARK
Author, *Raising Sinners*
Co-host, The Wonder Podcast &
Raising Sinners Podcast

The Pivot is an encouraging testimony of how we can respond in a Godly way when life doesn't look like we think it should. Sharing her powerful story of healing and restoration, Becky illustrates through scripture how we can choose to believe God when we don't understand our circumstances. Extremely well written and insightful, I highly recommend!

JEN SHERMAN
The Bookish Blonde

I clung to the pages of *The Pivot*, not because I wanted more story, but more of Jesus. I longed to be reminded that our God remains faithful in the darkest of nights. Becky shares unfathomable parts of her story with delicacy of detail yet bold authority of gospel truth. This book is a needed, and timely, reminder to walk in the light and receive the grace we are freely offered by a kind and good Father.

TERRI FLANNAGAN
Co-Founder, Ember CLT
Chief Strategist, Flannagan Consulting

If you've ever experienced loss (that's all of us!), this book is for you. We can all relate to Becky's story as we've all had moments of wanting to choose escape rather than courage and faith. Not only does Becky express her journey beautifully, but she incorporates truth from God's Word which has the power to pull us out of the pit and set our feet back on the rock. This book offers tremendous hope not because Becky in and of herself found healing, but because the Holy Spirit worked a miracle in her heart. And He can do the same for you.

HOLLY SHIVERS
Author, *I Can Learn to Pray* &
I Can Learn the Bible

Becky Leach gracefully invites us to sit with her in the tension between trauma and healing. . . the sacred space of *The Pivot*. Throughout her journey of profound suffering, Becky faithfully points us to Jesus. This book will leave you encouraged and full of belief in the God who loves us beyond measure.

HOLLY KNIGHT
Worship Leader
Author, *Stubborn Obedience*

I had the honor and privilege of being in the front seat with Becky as she experienced this journey. The words written in this book will cause you to experience victory in your own life as you see the realization that God is really good, even in unbelievable circumstances. He is always faithful!

CHRISSIE DUNHAM
Co-host, The Wonder Podcast +
Raising Sinners Podcast

Becky's vulnerability inspires courage and is contagious! While realizing complete wholeness comes when we get to heaven, she invites you to join her on her healing journey.

AMY FORD
President of Embrace Grace
Author, *Help Her Be Brave* +
A Bump in Life

ISBN 978-0-578-37574-8

THE PIVOT

BELIEVING GOD WHEN YOU REALLY, REALLY, DON'T WANT TO

BECKY LEACH

For The Seven:
Thank you for believing
with and for me when I
couldn't do it myself.

table of
CONTENTS

FOREWORD

There were ten thousand women in attendance at the Pink Impact conference where I was speaking. An interviewer asked me questions on stage about the history of Embrace Grace, the ministry God had given me a vision for at the very same Pink Impact conference many years before; a ministry that helps women with unexpected pregnancies.

As the interview wrapped up, the hostess thanked me for being a guest when I had a sudden stirring in my heart. The Lord prompted me to say *one more thing* before I walked off the stage.

I said, "There are ten thousand women in this arena which means about 2,500 of you have experienced an abortion. I really feel like the Lord wants me to say something to you ladies. He wants to start the healing process in your heart this weekend at this event. Many of you feel like you are disqualified from ministry, but God wants you to know that He qualifies you. You are an overcomer, and we overcome through Jesus and by sharing our story. Your story can help save lives! He loves you so much. Just open your heart to Him."

We had two Embrace Grace vendor booths at this arena, one on each end. As I closed the interview from the stage, our team quickly made their way back to our areas.

When the session released, women began flooding our booths. Many were inspired by the ministry and wanted to see how they could get involved by starting a group at their own church.

But what I could not get over were the hundreds of women with mascara smeared around their eyes because they had been crying so hard. Each of them looked into my eyes with that look, and I just *knew*. They didn't have to say a word.

They had experienced an abortion.

There is one woman I will never forget. She and her two sisters were wearing matching hot pink t-shirts that they'd made for the conference, and they looked as if they had expected a light-hearted, energetic weekend together. But God had different plans. More than fun, He wanted her to be free.

She had been so moved by my message that her sisters almost had to hold her up as she walked up to the booth. When they approached, one of them said quietly, "Our sister was touched by what you said today. She asked us to bring her over to meet you. She's really emotional and having a hard time talking."

It was a long time before she could say what she wanted. Finally, she looked up at me with a tear-drenched face and forced out a whisper with intensity. She asked, "Do you mean to tell me that God can use me?"

The thought had never crossed her mind. The pain, grief and regret of her abortion decision, whether it was by her own choice or a choice that had been forced upon her, fueled her feelings of unworthiness. But that day, something changed inside of her. A pivot in her heart was happening and a shift in her perspective. A new hope was rising, and she began to dream about the possibility of making a difference in the world, despite the pain from her past. She was making the choice to believe that God was her Comforter and that there could be purpose in her pain. She was making the choice to believe His words in Romans 8:28 that say, "And we know that God causes everything to work together for the good of those who love God and are called according to his purpose for them."

While working and speaking for Embrace Grace, and sharing my own story of unexpected seasons in my life filled with trials, hurts and injustices, I've had so many women wait their turn to speak to me afterward only to whisper in my ear a "me too" story. I've heard traumatic stories of neglect, death of loved ones, end of marriages, life-altering accidents, any and all forms of abuse and assault along with many other life experiences that bring grief and pain.

We all have some kind of hurt or trauma that we have walked through, some more painful than others. Sometimes the stories of our heartache are too hard to say out loud, but God knows each and every one. The pain that we experience on this earth sometimes feels like more than we can bear, but we were never meant to carry it alone.

It is not by accident that you got your hands on this book. Whether someone gave it to you or you were drawn to the subject matter or author and purchased it on your own, this is a *now word* that God has for you. Becky doesn't sugar coat or minimize trauma in any way. She has walked through hard and painful seasons herself, some she experienced even as she was writing this book, and she openly shares about her struggles with doubt and hurt along the way. Becky's vulnerability inspires courage and is contagious! While realizing complete wholeness comes when we get to heaven, she invites you to join her on her healing journey knowing that our only choice here on earth is whether we will believe God in the meantime.

My prayer is that as you read the pages of this book, you will open your heart to a new perspective and outlook moving forward. Not to try to forget or pretend the painful event never happened, but to pivot your mindset and believe that God is who He says He is. He called us to be free ... and free people, free people.

Amy Ford
President of Embrace Grace
Author + Speaker

AUTHOR'S NOTE

Hey girl, can we have a little chat before we get started? I think it's important for you to know up front that although I am a victim of abuse, this is not a book *about* abuse. Sure, it includes parts of my recovery, but if anything, it's a book about the relationship I desperately wanted that God refused to restore for me.

But it's also a story of survival. Of putting one foot in front of the other, but not knowing what the next step would actually be.

It's a story of forgiveness. Of choosing to believe that Jesus forgave *me*, so I am somehow able to forgive my abuser. . . even if he doesn't deserve it.

It's a story of God's faithfulness to my family, and our tireless efforts to choose him repeatedly. Even when it hurt, even when we questioned his plan, even when we felt alone, angry, and heart broken.

But above all, it's a story of gut-wrenching doubt and

supernatural belief. Of asking God, "What the heck is going on?" Then choosing to believe he is good anyway.

And although I hope that each of you will find a place among these pages, I feel the need to write a special message to my fellow victims of abuse as we get started.

To my strong survivor friends: You are amazing. You are warrior women who have come out on the other side of the unthinkable. *There is hope for you here.*

If you are reading this, you have already decided that *you* are worth fighting for—that *your faith* is worth fighting for. And no matter what your background is, no matter where you come from or how bad it has gotten, I want you to know that God's plan for you is *still* good.

Scripture is clear that he has a purpose for your life and he is able to redeem the heartache you have walked through. Maybe today will be an easy day, maybe it will be an emotional day, or maybe this will be the day you decide to finally address what happened to you all those years ago.

But maybe you simply need a friend to come up next to you and remind you that this was, and *never* will be, your fault.

It doesn't matter what you were wearing, what you said, what you drank, where you were—someone taking advantage of you, hitting you, spewing hateful things at you will absolutely never be your fault.

If you're anything like me, you can never hear that enough, so I'll say it one more time. This was not your fault. There is nothing to be ashamed of and nothing to be accountable for. You are welcomed here, seen here, loved here.

And with that said, if you, or someone you know is currently in an abusive situation, please reach out for help.

- National Domestic Abuse Hotline: 800-799-7233
- National Child Advocacy Centers: www.nationalcac.org/find-a-cac/
- The Salvation Army Transitional Shelters: www.salvationarmyusa.org/usn/stop-domestic-abuse/

Whatever your story is, I am thankful that the following pages get to be a part of it. I am constantly praying that they will bless you, encourage you, inspire you, and challenge you.

Now, let's get started.

PART ONE

01 | IT STARTS WITH A THING

We all have a thing.

A thing that whispers to us in the middle of the night. Whether it's that choice we made back in high school, the betrayal of a spouse years ago, or the middle of the night phone call we never expected to receive.

It's the same thing that the enemy so often uses against us when we're feeling most vulnerable, most weary, most stressed out, or most lonely.

My thing is sexual assault.

As a preteen and well into my teenage years, I was repeatedly molested by my father.

That's right, I just came out and said it. Truth be told, I compartmentalized it as best as I could for the next twenty years until the fall of 2017 when my body couldn't hold the secret any longer. It literally felt as if my bones were caving in on themselves while spontaneously combusting at the same time. Panic attacks, nightmares, and what was said to be "chronic stress" by two different doctors eventually forced me into a counselor's office for the first time, albeit reluctantly.

And in January of 2018, against a lifetime of my best effort, my deep, dark secret spilled out into the life that I knew, never to be contained again.

What has followed is years of learning how to deal with the aftermath. Learning how *not* to listen to the whispers inside my head but instead to the still small voice inside the deepest part of my heart—the Holy Spirit.

There were moments when I felt I had moved an elephant off my chest, and others when putting one foot in front of the other seemed impossible.

But what I've learned through all the highs, the lows, and the in-betweens is that God is still the God he says he is. Despite how I might feel, despite what I might see, and despite what my circumstances are telling me in the present.

MY QUESTION IS GOING TO BE THIS: DO YOU HAVE A THING?

So, my question is going to be this: Do you have a thing? Maybe you're not sure what it is yet. Maybe you're unsure of how you got to this exact point in your life, but you know that there is some thing happening inside of you here.

Some thing that is preventing you from living full and free in the abundant grace of Jesus.

Let's be honest, most people set out thinking life is going to look one way only to run into twists and turns, roadblocks, and speed bumps along the way. And maybe that's you. Maybe you're sitting here thinking, "There's got to be more to life than this," and I am here to holler back at you, "You're so right, there is!"

But how to get there? That's a whole adventure in and of itself, one that may be full of even more ups and downs, but the result is breathtaking freedom in Christ. The result is "living your best life" even in the heartache. The result is contentment in chaos, peace in tragedy, resolve in the consequences, and I hope that you're here for it.

Because I believe that if we, a generation of women, could figure out how to show up in our lives fully free, fully present, fully here with and for Jesus, our entire world could change. And I so desperately want that. For myself, for my family, but also for you.

This is the reason I share my story and have shared it countless times—because I so deeply want you to experience the freedom that Jesus Christ died to give us, not just for eternity, but for living our life right now.

There are a few things I want you to know about me before we even get started, and the first one is this: I'm a pretty messed up gal. I sin and make terrible mistakes—like, on the daily. I say things I shouldn't and most definitely *think* things I shouldn't. I get angry and lash out and want things that aren't mine to have.

The second thing is that at the end of the day, despite all the mistakes and mishaps that I make, I deeply love Jesus and want to spend the rest of my life chasing after him. It's not easy, but I have seen what life with him is like, and I want it desperately. With every word spilled across these pages before you, my prayer is that God's redemptive power, despite my overwhelmingly flawed humanity, shines through.

I HAD TO CHOOSE TO BELIEVE HIM. IT'S AS SIMPLE AND COMPLICATED AS THAT.

A while back my friend Magen asked, "Becky, how do you reconcile a good God with a God who allowed you to be traumatized in such a horrific way?" She was working on a sermon and having trouble putting the obvious, but difficult answer, into words.

I've had to answer this question in some of my darkest moments. I've had to reconcile what I know to be true about the God I love and serve with what I've experienced in my life. I've had to ask the hard questions like, "Why would God allow this to happen to me," which would always lead me back to, "But why *not* me?"

My reply to Magen came out before I even had time to think about it. It was short but profound.

"I guess I just came to a point when I had to choose to

believe him. It's as simple and complicated as that."

And that's what this book is about: the lessons I have learned by believing God when I just really, *really* didn't want to. The lessons I'm still learning when I still don't want to.

The truth is that life will never be neat and tidy, and despite our collective efforts and prayers, rarely does it end like one of those feel-good Hallmark movies that we all know and love. Instead, it's quite complicated, sometimes lonely, and, at times, disappointing.

Why?

Because we live in a broken world where bad things happen to people who love God and people who love God make mistakes. *Lots of them.* And even though I have no idea what category you might fall into at this very moment, I do know this:

Jesus loves you.

Not only does he love you, but he has plans for your life. Plans that are good and wonderful and full. No matter where you are, what you've done, or how broken your heart is right now, Jesus offers peace, love, mercy, and yes, even joy.

So before you write me off because you just want to stay stuck in your grief for a little while longer, I want to tell you this third and final thing.

I will always be honest with you.

Life just flat-out sucks sometimes and it's certainly not fair. In the pages that follow, I'm going to open the hard parts of my heart so you can hear someone say, "Yeah, you're right. That is extremely difficult. I'm sorry that happened to you. I'm sorry for what you've walked through. It's okay to not be okay."

I won't ever tell you to get over your hurt. I won't demand that you figure out how to be happy, move on already, or just, for the love of God, "choose joy." I have never been able to do that myself, no matter how many well-meaning people encouraged me to. My inability to get over the trauma in my life caused me to wrestle with this thought: Maybe we aren't supposed to shove our feelings and less than ideal circumstances into a box. Instead, maybe we just need to pivot.

In the book of Psalms, we repeatedly see David (and the other psalmists) cry out to the Lord in lament. David begs God to intervene when an enemy army pursues him. He cries out asking hard questions like, why was the other side winning. He begs God to pour out his vengeance and wrath on his enemies! He pleads for forgiveness out of gut-wrenching repentance.

The Bible is full of heartache.

But there is *always* a pivot from heartache to what is true about God.

In Psalm 31 David begins, "Be gracious to me, Lord for I am in distress; my eye is wasted away from grief; my soul and my body too. For my life is spent with sorrow and my years with sighing; my strength has failed because of my guilt and my body has wasted away." (Psalm 31:9-10)

Girl, now that's some grief!

A mere five verses later though, he writes, "But as for me, I trust in you, Lord, I say, 'You are my God.'" (Psalm 31:14)

He chose to pivot.

He chose trust.

He chose *belief.*

I think sometimes I would become frustrated with the "feeling" of faith. When we become believers, especially those of us who began a relationship with the Lord at such a young age, we get attached to this idea that faith is something we should feel. It's the "camp high" or the soft heart or the prayerful attitude that we think we should constantly have as believers. It's the thought that we should never ever question God.

FAITH IS A DAILY DECISION TO BELIEVE GOD DESPITE OUR CIRCUMSTANCE.

But what if faith is not a one-time choice? What if our faith is the daily decision to believe God—despite our circumstances, good or bad?

In his second letter to the Corinthians, Paul describes faith as a walk, not simply a moment in time, not something we possess forever. He says, "So we are always of good courage. We know that while we are at home in the body we are away from the Lord, for we walk by faith and not by sight." (2 Corinthians 5:6-7)

Walking is an action, just as faith is an action. The Greek word Paul uses here for walk is peripatéō which means "to make one's way, to progress."[1] Progress in our faith is not indicative of standing still, is it? It's moving forward, consistently pivoting from what we feel to what we know.

I'm not asking you to be fake or pretend your ache isn't real, wherever it's coming from, and I'm not suggesting that pivoting will make your problems go away, or even that it will make it feel better.

But pivoting is the choice that gives us freedom in our faith. It's the choice that leads to the healing, the surrender, or the breakthrough that we're looking for. And it's the choice we're going to have to make again and again and again if we want to continue to walk in our faith.

So, are you ready to believe God?

It's often said that life is a series of choices. Sometimes we make good ones and sometimes, if you're anything like me, we make bad ones. The choice that consistently affects our lives as followers of Christ though is whether we will believe. Whether we believe God to be who he claims to be in the Bible. Whether we believe that we are daughters of a living and breathing almighty Father God. Whether we believe that God's promises of the Bible are also his promises for us. Whether we believe he has good for us, plans for us, a future for us.

All these beliefs are choices we have to make on repeat while experiencing the constant highs and lows of life. Our faith grows exponentially when we choose him despite how we feel and despite what we see.

I so desperately want you to know and understand that your own journey from doubt to belief is not uncommon, it does not mean you're a "bad Christian," or that you have too little faith. It means you are human, and you will flounder and fail more times than you'll care to admit. *We all will.* And so my hope here is to encourage you as you learn to pivot by sharing my stories while I come alongside of you, link arms, and walk forward together.

I want to kick it all off with my very favorite passage of scripture (which I'll probably share a hundred times before this is all done). This is the Message version because it's the

> **OUR FAITH GROWS EXPONETIALLY WHEN WE CHOOSE GOD DESPITE HOW WE FEEL.**

pep talk that we all need as we learn to pivot.

> Do you see what this means—all these pioneers
> who blazed the way, all these veterans cheering us
> on? It means we'd better get on with it. Strip down,
> start running—and never quit! No extra spiritual
> fat, no parasitic sins. Keep your eyes on Jesus, who
> both began and finished this race we're in. Study
> how he did it. Because he never lost sight of where
> he was headed—that exhilarating finish in and with
> God—he could put up with anything along the way:
> Cross, shame, whatever. And now he's there, in the
> place of honor, right alongside God. When you find
> yourselves flagging in your faith, go over that story
> again, item by item, that long litany of hostility he
> plowed through. That will shoot adrenaline into your
> souls! (Hebrews 12:1-3, MSG)

In 2018, I chose to believe God, to shift my focus from the world back to the Lord, who he is, and who he said I was. It didn't come easy, but no one knows that better than I do. Because at thirty-five years old, my life was about to turn upside down. For better or worse, I was going to find out who my God really was.

It was my chance to believe.

02 | THE SECRETS WE KEEP

I was probably seventeen when I finally realized that what my dad was doing to me was wrong. That the secret "lessons" he had been teaching me about my body since I was twelve, in the privacy of his bedroom, weren't actually lessons at all. That the man who was supposed to protect, love, care for, and nurture me was, in fact, the one who was *hurting* me.

The lies about my situation ran rampant through my head.

Surely he didn't mean to hurt me.

He doesn't know any better; this is probably how he was raised.

I wonder if someone hurt him like this; I feel sorry for him.

Becky, you're not a baby; you could have walked away, but you didn't.

Your mom will never speak to you again.

You'll lose everybody. You'll get kicked out. You'll be all alone.

But what could I do about it now? It was done.

I loved him. Of course I loved him; he was my dad. I so wanted his stamp of approval and despite all the evidence to the contrary, I convinced myself he loved me too. So I shut up, kept it to myself, and devised a plan in my head. I avoided situations to be alone with him, I would frantically seek out reasons to be out of the house if my mom wasn't home.

I would ask friends to come over, find dates to go on, errands to run. All to avoid telling the truth... even to myself.

I COULD SURVIVE MORE IF I HAD ALREADY SURVIVED ALL THIS.

It wasn't fail-proof, but it was at least better. Because if it stopped happening—or, didn't happen as much—then it would all be okay. I would be okay. I could survive more if I had already survived all of this. So, I thought, if I could just hold it all together for a few more years, I would go to college, have my own space, and all would be well so no one would ever need to know.

No one needed to know about the tears I cried alone in my bed at night.

No one needed to know how desperate I was just to lock the bathroom door.

No one needed to know how the smell of Icy Hot made me vomit.

No one needed to know that the word "prude" sent shivers down my spine.

No one needed to know the innocence lost, the exposure I had as a mere child or what I accepted in an effort to seek love and approval.

Obviously, I couldn't have been more wrong.

My mother has asked me since if I hated high school. My answer is a resounding 'no' because it definitely wasn't *all* bad.

It was during high school that I went on a first date with Jeff Leach. I was nervous because, well, he was my *friend* I'd had a crush on for a while, but our signals kept getting crossed. Either I was dating someone else, or he was, but finally things clicked.

Sparks ignited. Years later—even to this day—I would tell my kids that the first time I saw him, I knew I would marry him, and he would say the same thing too.

Jeff and I went to different high schools, but being the ladies' man he denies he was, he knew a lot of the girls from my high school. One girl in particular, a friend of mine, asked him to go to our homecoming as her date. I knew he would be there, and, against my best efforts, I couldn't help myself from counting down the minutes until my date and I were finished with dinner so I could get that dance he had promised me.

My date and I barely made it before the doors closed for the night. As custom, I danced the first slow dance with my date, an old friend, but it was official: I had spotted Jeff. Moments later, after losing our original dates, while dancing the night away in a hotel ballroom crowded with hundreds of teenagers clothed in sweat and unbelievable amounts of hairspray, he asked me on our very first date.

My life has, thankfully, never been the same.

On October 24, 1998, the doorbell rang around six. Jeff introduced himself to my mom, and she proceeded to take a million pictures with what I'm convinced was the very first, and very large, digital camera. I wore my trusty boot cut black pants with a boxy (you could say it was ugly) gray sweater I'd purchased at Old Navy earlier that day. He wore khakis and a sweater vest that he had borrowed from our worship minister at church. The picture is funny—two kids who didn't know how in love they were yet, being awkward and nervous as things began rapidly growing from friendship into relationship.

He took me to La Hacienda for Mexican food and then to his school's Sadie Hawkins dance. I wasn't quite aware of this at the time, but he'd been asked to the dance by a few other girls. I knew literally no one at his school, so I felt like a fish out of water.

Jeff went all out and took me to 7-11 afterwards for Slurpees. He showed me how to mix the cherry and the Coke together in the most perfect proportion. (This is still his go-to treat, by the way.) The way I acted, you'd have thought he invented this concept. We drove to a new park behind the local library and it was there that he asked me to be his girlfriend. Actually, that's not an accurate telling of the story. He said, "I'd like for you to be my girlfriend," to which I responded, "Well, you can ask me anytime."

I had never been more comfortable or at ease with anyone in my life—not even my girlfriends. When I was younger, our family moved around every few years as my father climbed the corporate ladder. I was constantly meeting new friends, but somehow, he made me feel like we had known each other forever. He was kind, strong, passionate, and he loved me. He soon became my safe place.

As our dating progressed, we, like many teenagers, were on the phone constantly—even late at night after my phone curfew. We'd stay on the phone for hours, sometimes until we fell asleep. It was young love in its purest form, talking about everything and nothing all at the same time.

I was absolutely an open book, as was he. He could "ask me anything," as I often told him. Maybe he didn't ask me the right question, or maybe I just wasn't ready to give an answer.

Either way, I told him everything *except* what was

happening to me when he'd drop me off after a movie. Everything *except* the darkest part of my life. Looking back on it, I don't believe I intentionally withheld the information, but instead was convinced it was so separate from the rest of my life that he didn't want or need to know.

> # LITTLE DID I KNOW THAT THE SLOWER PACE WOULD MAKE THE LORD'S VOICE EVEN CLEARER.

Jeff and I got married at twenty-two and had our oldest son at twenty-five. Jeff was in law school, and I worked full time as an interior designer with a firm I loved. We served at our local church where Jeff taught our Sunday school class, and I taught kindergarten with a group of girlfriends. We did Bible studies and took mission trips and said yes when others said no. We loved God and our marriage was good and our family was growing quickly.

We moved into our first house in the suburbs when our oldest was nearly two. I was so thankful to be "out of the city" where it was quieter, and life was slower. Little did I know that the slower pace would make the Lord's voice even clearer.

On October 31, 2009, I started in my prayer journal, "Lord. I don't even know where to begin. I don't think I've ever written this on paper before. I don't think I've ever talked to you about this before. My heart is heavy."

We were praying about growing our family, and I very much wanted a daughter, as did Jeff. The mere idea of it made me think about my relationship with my father, what her relationship with Jeff would be, and what I certainly did not want it to look like. Like so many victims, having children puts childhood trauma in a different perspective. It brings it to the surface, it reframes it, it gives you context outside of the vacuum you experienced it in.

I remember thinking that it was a huge risk to write it down like that. As I would write about it more, I only referred to it as "the thing with my dad" for fear of it getting picked up and read. But part of me hoped that would happen, saving me the impending fear of bringing it up in a conversation.

I continued in that journal entry, "Lord, I am struggling. Take me through the healing process. I've never really begun to deal with this—please help me start now. Help me to forgive myself. Help me to trust Jeff, even with this information—Father, this is so painful. My heart has never ached like this before. I need you to carry me through this process. Help me. Help me please."

The very next day I mentioned it out loud. It was a Sunday afternoon, and we had just put Brady down for a nap and sat down to watch the Dallas Cowboys destroy (or lose to) the Seahawks on television. Chips and salsa were out on the coffee table; I had a giant Troy Aikman jersey on because it's football and we do football up right in our house.

It was sunny outside, we were doing my favorite thing

in the world, and I started crying.

God had been working on my heart for several weeks now to tell Jeff—to say the things I had hidden from him our entire relationship. For years I hadn't thought about what I went through as a child, a teen. I had become a master compartmentalizer, shoving any feeling or thought associated with my father down deep and to the side. But now that I was a parent, things were beginning to bubble up to the surface, especially feelings of shame and guilt.

How could you have let this happen? Why wouldn't you just walk away? Why didn't you tell someone at the time? No one will believe you now!

I have never been good at hiding my feelings, but hiding *that*? I had always been good at that. Until that moment.

"Jeff, at halftime, could we talk?" I blurted it out, almost surprising myself.

I honestly couldn't hold it in a second longer, so I was grateful he took one look at me, knew it was serious, and pushed pause on the game—something we don't take lightly at the Leach house.

I couldn't get the words out. They were begging to be released, but I didn't even know what to say. I didn't have words to describe what had happened. Did he molest me? Did he manipulate me? Did he bribe me? Did he assault me?

So I took the easier road, leaving it at a very generalized statement like, "When I was younger, something happened with my dad." There shouldn't have been a period on the end of that sentence, but that's where I left it. I wouldn't tell him the end of the story for a long time.

He could tell I was upset. He knew it was serious. And he could have pushed me. He could have pried and begged it to come out of me. But I wasn't ready.

So he did the only thing he knew to do and said, "Would you like to talk about it?"

I remember that moment like it was yesterday. My body was screaming at me—*yes, talk about it.* But my mind was screaming just a little bit louder—*no, he will never understand.*

I had just thrown a silent grenade into the middle of our marriage without either of us knowing how to deal with it. We were young parents, still freshly married. As much as I knew he was safe, I also didn't know he would *stay* safe. So I said no, I didn't want to talk about it, but just wanted him to know it was on my heart.

Years later, it would come spilling out of me beyond my control.

Years later, my life would come crashing down around me leaving only rubble on the outside of a broken-down frame God would then have to rebuild.

Years later, I would choose to believe that God was walking with me the entire time.

03 | AN INTERVENTION

Finally in 2018, I went to a counselor for the panic attacks I eventually had because I kept shutting my body up. I sat on a couch on a dark and rainy Thursday morning in downtown Dallas and told her the thing I had never dared to speak aloud—the same something that had "happened with my dad."

My sweet counselor looked at me gently after I described the situation in the most general, high-level way possible and said, "Becky, you were molested, you know that, right?"

Was I? That couldn't be right.

Because if I were molested that means my dad could go to jail. And if my dad could go to jail, my parents could get divorced. And if my parents got divorced, that would make it my fault. And if that were my fault—well, I couldn't possibly live with myself.

So much has happened since that day. Heartache, consequences, change. You'll find much of that woven throughout this book—because it was in this heartache that God showed up and showed off. I learned that no matter the circumstance, I could believe him.

I told Jeff the story soon after that appointment. He had a hint that the "something with my dad" was bigger than he realized when, weeks before my first appointment, he found me outside of a New York City restaurant struggling to catch my breath. I was having my first panic attack. He looked at me softly, and on the street across from Central Park he said, "maybe it's time you see someone."

Soon after I let him in, I decided I *still* didn't want to tell anyone else. Certainly Jeff was the only one who absolutely needed to know so that I could start the healing process. He was the only one I felt I was lying to, that I was keeping a secret from. I still had one other problem though: not leaving my father alone with my kids, niece, or nephews.

I dreaded this conversation above all the things. It kept me up nearly every night for two months.

How in the world would I address the fact that the man who was supposed to love and protect me for eighteen years did the opposite? What if he denied it? What if he diminished it?

Now that someone had come into my life and said,

"Becky—this isn't a gray area. This is an *actual* crime," I could no longer not see it that way. I could no longer shove it to the side, push it deep down, smile, and get on with it. I couldn't make nice when he hugged my daughter . . . or me. There was no putting this genie back in the bottle.

> **I WAS NO LONGER NORMAL, AND MY CIRCUMSTANCES WEREN'T EITHER.**

A few weeks later my mom called to tell me that my grandfather had passed away suddenly. My grandmother has been in poor health for many years, along with my aunt, but my grandfather? He rarely had health problems. She was in Tyler with the rest of the family and asked if I could be with my dad, maybe take him something to eat and make sure he was alright.

Normally, this is my life's calling—to help and serve others. Under other circumstances, I would have jumped at the chance to console someone in their grief, prepared a four-course meal with tons of leftovers and directions on how to reheat everything in the microwave—enough for days.

But I was no longer normal, and my circumstances weren't either.

I sat down in my back yard behind a tree and sobbed until my head hurt. I screamed into the air. Not because I was sick over losing my grandfather, but because I could no longer be the daughter I once was, no matter how I addressed this thing. And because now, my father was not the father I thought he once was.

Thankfully my rock star of a husband took care of everything. He texted my mom that we already had dinner plans, then went straight to the grocery store and bought a rotisserie chicken, some root beer and maybe a microwave dinner or two. He let himself into my parents' house, just down the street from ours, and stuck everything in the fridge. Then he came home and took me and the kids out to dinner.

I was officially broken. I knew that much. It was an eye-opening moment, knowing that I couldn't fake it anymore. And as much as I really wanted to pretend everything was OK, I knew something was going to have to give. The dam was about to break, and I didn't want to drown.

While at dinner that night, my sister (and youngest sibling), texted me. She had known I was going to counseling, although she had no clue what for. She typed, "I know you are really upset, and I know it isn't all about Grandaddy. Whenever you're ready to talk about it, I would really like to know. I'm here for you."

Jeff read it, took a sip of his drink, gently reached for my hand and softly said, "Becky, it's time."

———————

That Sunday night, after our kids went to bed, Katie

showed up with a bottle of wine and a box of Kleenex. With her husband on speaker phone, Jeff prayed for us and turned it over to me. From start to finish, I told my story. Of how it started and how it got out of control before I was old enough to know what was happening. I talked about how much I loved our dad and was worried about what this would do to our family. I said I was sorry about a million times, I told them I understood if they didn't believe me, and then I closed my eyes and braced myself for their response.

After a long pause and a deep breath, my brother-in-law, Trent, said with a hint of firmness in his voice, "Becky— no matter what happens from here, you are not alone. We are behind you and with you in this."

A fresh wave of relief washed over me from head to toe. Another load had been lifted. And as much as I hate to admit it, Jeff had known all along I would feel this way once I let her in. I can't keep my heart hidden once it cracks open, especially from those I love the most.

Now it was the four of us who knew about this "thing with my dad." We had more to discuss, and I had more questions to answer. Several days later we attended the funeral in east Texas. My entire family was going to be there, and it would be the first time I had seen my dad since bringing this darkness into the light. I grinned, bore it, and did my best to stay in a corner away from my dad.

As much as I prayed we would end up in a group dinner situation, we ended up at Chuy's in a round booth with only the eight of us. I sat quietly between Jeff and my sister while my dad sat across from us. It felt as if there was a mile between us when in reality it was just a basket of chips and a side of salsa.

Someone asked our dad how he was holding up through all of this and how our grandmother was doing. He quickly shared that "family drama" was causing some additional issues. Drama that we had never heard about before. People were threatening not to come to the funeral and others were coming but not speaking to each other. It was all a bit complicated, like it is in most families.

If they only knew the family drama brewing underneath the surface.

THIS IS THE STORY GOD CREATED YOU TO TELL.

We called a "sibling meeting" after the funeral to tell my brother, Cameron, and his wife, Lauren. I'm not sure what they were expecting to hear, but what I said wasn't it. I valued Cam's approval, as we had grown up close but walked through a period of mild estrangement in college. I braced myself for his response, his disappointment, his doubt. Again, I was met with the same resolve, compassion, and heartbreak.

My brother hugged me tightly before leaving and said, "This is the story God created you to tell."

But how would we now move forward? Since my siblings knew and supported me without a doubt, I felt strong enough to go to battle. For our family, for myself, for

> **I KNEW THIS WAS GOD'S TIMING AND HIS WILL. AND NOW, THIS WAS MY ACT OF OBEDIENCE.**

my parents. Over the next few days, my siblings and I shot a lot of emails back and forth, most of which I still have saved in my inbox.

Eventually we decided that we needed to confront our dad, but we weren't sure how. Would it just be Jeff and me? Would it include my siblings? Should we have a counselor there? How should we tell my mom—should we *even* tell my mom? My heart felt unsettled, but at the same time, God's peace was underneath it all. I knew that this was his timing, this was his will, and now, this was my act of obedience.

––––––––––

At some point on the morning of March 7, 2018, only a few days later, I received a series of texts from my father about getting together for lunch. He missed me, he said, and the flimsy barrier I had haphazardly built around my heart crashed.

I cried, went for a walk, took a shower, one deep breath, and then another. My heart felt as if it were going to pound out of my chest. My head throbbed from the crying; my face remained flush with anxiety. I sat down with my Bible and made every attempt to pray. I wish I could say it was the first thing I did, but in truth, it was the only thing left to do.

Words failed me.

Thoughts shamed me.

Heartbreak swallowed me.

I honestly don't remember what I prayed. I don't even remember if I read any Scripture from my open Bible. All I remember was a holy resolve rising inside of me. *God was with me.* He would fight for me. And suddenly, I knew that today, I would break free once and for all.

I pulled out my phone and with shaking hands shot a text to my siblings and our spouses:

"Today has to be the day. Can y'all get over here tonight?" Everyone quickly said yes. We hopped on a conference call and discussed it. They moved their days around. They got babysitters. They ate dinner early, decided to fight traffic, and canceled evening plans so that this would be the day I could finally let go. We were *all* ready, but none more than me. I had carried this weight for twenty-three years. It was time to shed it.

My brother, Cameron, asked my parents if he could meet with them to talk through a struggle. We decided not to call a "family meeting," since we'd receive a flurry of texts asking what it was about. So Cam, acting like the boss he is, took this on for himself so I wouldn't have to.

The rest of the day was all about going through the motions, trying to survive until we left. We were staying with friends at the time because our kitchen was being remodeled, (our timing is always good) so they provided distraction and encouragement. They were the only ones outside of our family who knew what was going on.

Jeff brought home tacos for our little sister family. We served ourselves and sat down at the dining room table while Jeff sent the kids upstairs to eat and watch TV—a treat in the eyes of any kid. The four of us sat in silence. I was starving but my nerves wouldn't let me eat a dang thing, tears welling up in my throat.

We tried our best to make small talk, but it was no use. Our friend Craig eventually asked if he could pray over us, so we joined hands, and through tears, he asked God to do what only he could do—restore.

WE KNEW WHAT GOD WAS CAPABLE OF.

Seven thirty rolled around. We said goodnight to our kids, hugged Craig and Julie, then drove over to our house covered in plastic sheeting and brown paper taped to the floor. Jeff and I sat under the bright overhead lighting quietly holding hands as we waited for my siblings to arrive.

The smell of paint was fresh, but not overwhelming. I looked around feeling as messy as our home. Furniture was piled into the middle of each room, the windows were taped off, the counters covered.

I sighed, but then a flicker of hope ignited my weary heart. *When we move back home,* I thought, *all of this mess will get put back together and wiped clean. And so will I.*

My siblings—my people—finally arrived and Cam hugged me tightly. As tears quietly slipped from his eyes and mine, he prayed over all six of us and over the conversation that was about to happen. We squeezed hands, passed tissues, and said "amen" again and again. Our hearts were after redemption, forgiveness, reconciliation, and freedom. We knew what God was capable of. We were handing it all to him, convinced he would show up.

Shortly afterward, three cars pulled up at my parents' home a short mile away, one behind another. It was chilly but not freezing, cloudy but not damp. Six car doors opened, breaking the quiet of the night, and six doors closed. Not a word uttered, only hands squeezed as we made our way to the door behind my not so little younger brother.

Here we go.

————————

Our dad answered.

I am convinced he knew exactly what was happening the moment he saw all six of us standing on his front porch. Moving quickly to the side, he silently let us all in one after another. He watched all of us closely, and I did my best not to make eye contact. If I looked at him, I would lose my confidence. I was sure of it.

Maybe this isn't the right thing. He's my dad. Am I about to ruin his life? What about my mom's? Why am

I doing this again? Life can just keep going on. Things were fine as they were. No one else has to know. Let's turn around. Stop it. Let's just stop it.

I COULDN'T GO BACK, THAT MUCH WAS CLEAR.

I hugged my mom tightly. The look of confusion on her face broke my heart in two. *What if she doesn't believe me? She's going to have to choose. Him or me. What if she chooses him? What do I do if I lose both of my parents in one night?*

We exchanged pleasantries but quickly and quietly took seats around the living room coffee table. No drinks were offered and the snacks my mother had lovingly prepared sat untouched on the kitchen island. Looking back, it felt like it all happened in slow motion. Cam, his wife Lauren, and my mom on one sofa with Jeff, my sister Katie, and I on the other. Trent, my brother-in-law, perched on the edge of the recliner closest to my sister as he reached over to squeeze her hand.

I was weary, and my heart was already shattered. I couldn't go back, that much was clear. Our father stood at the front of the room shifting his weight from one leg to another. (He's the only person in the world who can find a way to pace while standing in one place.)

My dad took a deep breath and spoke. "This looks like an intervention."

I'll never forget that phrase, not only because that's now how we refer to March 7th, but because that is nothing we wanted it to be. I had fervently prayed for a night of freedom, reconciliation, and truth telling. We *all* had. But there was nothing to intervene on. He assaulted me twenty years ago. Surely he wasn't still that same heartless and cruel person today.

No, this was never supposed to be an intervention.

Cam started.

He began with this, "I called this family meeting at someone else's request." My head hung low. *I can't believe this is happening. This is it.* I held my breath for as long as I could just so I felt in control of something.

"There is someone who has been deeply wronged in our family." He took a breath and shifted his focus from the entire room to one person. "Dad, by you."

My dad was still standing. At some point, Cam asked him to sit down.

"Our goal is reconciliation here, dad. Our goal is that we leave here stronger, even if a bit broken. We expect there to be a period of separation, but our sincere hope is that we will all eventually come back together. It's time to bring the darkness into the light, and that's exactly what we're going to do. So, dad, I wanted to give you a chance to make this wrong right. Is there anything you would like to say?"

He swallowed hard. My eyes remained fixed on my brother while my hand stayed solidly in Jeff's. There was no way I could even look in my dad's direction. *What if he doesn't say anything? What if he confesses to something else? What if he denies it and calls me crazy? What if . . .*

"Yes, I have wronged someone." The thickness of his voice filled the room. He looked at me with hollow eyes, a recognition of defeat. "That person is Becky."

My heart pounded. I thought this would feel different. By now I thought tears would be heaving poison out of my body. I thought he would deny it. I thought he would break down. I thought he would show remorse and beg for forgiveness.

I subtly nodded my head in acknowledgment of what he said.

> JUST BECAUSE GOD DOESN'T DO ALL THAT HE **COULD** DO, DOESN'T MEAN HE ISN'T DOING SOMETHING.

He then quickly admitted a shallow portion of what he did, apologized as best he could at the time, and tried to move us on out of there, claiming he did the best he knew how as a father.

This conversation will remain etched in our memories forever. It didn't go at all how I thought that it would, but God wove his compassion in and through that night more than I could ever recognize at the time. I always want to remember that I didn't have to say a word, that my abuse was validated in those moments, that I *did* get an apology, even if it wasn't sincere.

What I realized that night, and I still want you to see

today, is that just because God doesn't do all that he could do, doesn't mean he isn't right there doing something. He is working good we cannot yet see—protecting your heart and soul in ways that might not make sense in the moment.

Several years later, I look back through the tears, heartache, and confusion to see that despite it all, God was and is everything he said he would be. He was kind and merciful, just and sovereign. He not only protected my little family but my larger one too. He walked with us and in his timing he gave us peace that passes all understanding while he somehow intertwined joy with our heartbreak.

As much as I could have chosen *not* to see it, over the next several months—years, really—God taught me, ever so gently, to believe him. Even when—especially when—I didn't want to. And believe me, I wanted to remain stuck in the anger and what ifs many times. I still do sometimes. But every single time, he brings me back to the pivot.

That August, we took my whole family to the beach. My whole family, except my dad. By this point he had stopped pursuing us along with any sort of restoration. My parents were separated, and we were all desperate to begin healing. At the beach we could wash our sandals off, and take a break from the process for a bit.

Despite the crashing waves and sparkling sunshine, I wrestled with my grief and heartache, still asking God the hard questions. Why would he would allow like this to happen. Why not just say the word and fix it for us?

During that trip, I devoured the book of Psalms on a humid screened-in balcony with a cup of coffee each morning. In these raw poems, David honestly cried out to God—in pain, in grief, in fear, in repentance. He also asked God questions like why and how, questions summed up with "when will this end, Lord?"

I was in good company.

But then I noticed something new.

Every time David cried out, he pivoted. Sometimes it was quick and sometimes it happened eventually—but he always did it. He turned from his grief *back* to God. He turned from his sin *back* to grace. He turned from his fear back to the strength of God, from sadness back to the hope in God's sovereignty.

And I said to myself in those moments, "Maybe I should try that."

Enter *The Pivot*.

04 | THE PIVOT

I was talking with a friend about writing this book—writing about believing God. We discussed all of the decisions we make in different seasons of life, but each one can be wrapped in just one fundamental choice: Whether or not we will believe God, his promises, and his character.

"You know, Becky," she said. "I know you want to talk about believing God, but when I look at your life, I only see that it has not turned out like you expected—or really, even how you prayed it would."

And she's right.

On the outside looking in, our life might look wonderful. I have a supportive husband, three wonderful (but sometimes obnoxious) children, a circle of friends that I hold dear. But the reality I've never shied from is that life is not at all what I had hoped or expected or begged God for. Not by a long shot.

My parents were no longer together because of a secret I revealed. I don't have a relationship with my father, despite a longing for one. And now I'm dealing with the never-ending aftermath of trauma in my life, something that I know will never be "healed" this side of heaven.

So here I sit, now 39, still waiting. Waiting on healing and restoration, forgiveness, and justice. Waiting while knowing God *could* give me all these things with a word but hasn't yet and, maybe, never will.

> **WHAT DOES IT LOOK LIKE IF LIFE NEVER GETS WRAPPED UP IN THAT PRETTY LITTLE BOW?**

If you've picked up this book, I bet you're in this dark place too, waiting in your heartache and grief for God to show up and show off. And if you're not in this dark place today, maybe you've been there before. And based on my experience, I can honestly tell you that it doesn't always end up okay, but *you* can still be okay.

So often we read books that tell stories of believing God after the heartache is wrapped up in a neat little bow. Testimonies of faith shared after the miracle came, after the sickness was healed, after the restoration took place.

But what does it look like if life never gets wrapped up in that bow? What if God never gives us the "desires of our heart," or we never see the end of our wait? What do we do then?

We pivot.

Pivot. The dictionary offers many definitions of the word as well as many forms—pivotal, pivoting, finding a pivot. But the one I find the most interesting: a usually marked change.[1]

A *marked* change.

We have all experienced change in our lives at some point. Whether it's a season changing, a relationship changing, or the whole world changing, life is ever evolving, and we go along with it.

But *marked* change? That's interesting.

To me that suggests significance or intentionality behind that kind of change. When David pivoted in the Psalms, it was often an about-face, a total and complete redirection from where his thoughts were originally headed.

I noticed it first in the third psalm.

David starts, "O Lord, how many are my foes! Many are rising against me; many are saying of my soul, 'There is no salvation for him in God.'" (Psalm 3:1-2)

Have you ever felt this way? That the whole world is rising up against you? Jeff likes to tell me I'm dramatic sometimes—even though it doesn't get him very far—but a few seasons of my life have felt just like as this verse describes. Namely, campaigning with my husband.

I forgot to mention that Jeff holds a political office. It's not the thing I often lead with, but I do feel it's important to note that we have experienced the whole "many are rising against me" thing in real life.

The world flings so much criticism and judgment today, so much hate and bitterness. It can feel like the whole world is your enemy at any point. Whether it's politically, religiously, or just ideologically, we see the disagreement spewed out on the news and social media on a daily basis.

And although similar, this isn't exactly what was happening to David. Stick with me for just a second as I try to put Psalm 3 in context for you.

David wrote this while fleeing Jerusalem, his kingdom, for the Mount of Olives. Why? Because Absalom had been conspiring against him for a while. In fact, Scripture tells us that over four years before the actual coup, "Absalom stole the hearts of the men of Israel" by wooing them with phrases like, "If I were king . . ." (2 Samuel 15:6)

So yeah, David was in a bad spot because someone was trying to kick him out and take over. That someone had turned Israel against him, so much so that he was felt like he was beyond help in God. But what made it worse is that David *loved* this someone—his own flesh and blood. Absalom was his son.

I have three kids at home, one now a teenager, and

I completely understand the heartache of repeated and intentional disobedience by a child (or all of them). I have found it difficult to separate out my identity from their free will because I know God has and wants so much more for them than their disobedience.

So I can only imagine the complicated grief involved here. This isn't the kind of disobedience we deal with day to day. This isn't coming home and finding out that your kids didn't clean their room like you had requested. This is coming home and seeing your bags packed at a locked back door saying, "Don't come back here. Ever."

Now, that's heart-breaking.

And so David cried out to God. He lamented and wept and prayed.

> David went up the ascent of the Mount of Olives, weeping as he went, barefoot and with his head covered. And all the people who were with him covered their heads, and they went up, weeping as they went."(2 Samuel 15:30)

His heart was, understandably, in turmoil.

Maybe you've been here before. This psalm stuck out to me so much in 2018 because I felt like my heart was in this spot of telling God, "It feels like everyone is against me" even if they weren't.

I felt like I was too much for my friends. I felt like I was not enough for my kids. I felt abandoned by my father (which I was). I felt like I had betrayed my family. I felt ashamed but angry. I felt heartbroken and regretful.

There was so much going on for me emotionally. I quite literally felt the weight of the world on my shoulders as the family I knew had disintegrated to ashes before my eyes. And as much as I knew it wasn't my fault, I felt a thick layer of guilt surrounding it all. I completely identified with David here and paid close attention to what this "man after God's own heart" did next. (Acts 13:22)

"But you, O Lord, are a shield about me, my glory, and the lifter of my head." (Psalm 3:3)

The pivot.

Do you see the about-face? The complete 180 that David does during his weeping, heartsickness, and grief?

But you, O Lord . . .

He intentionally turned his thoughts from his circumstance to his creator, from fear to the Lord's protection, from grief to praise. This didn't come naturally; it didn't just happen, as indicated in this prayer by his use of the word *but*. This word suggests an actual choice.

And we see this choice made repeatedly in the Psalms.

While seeing the success of his enemies: "But let all who take refuge in you rejoice . . ." (Psalm 5:11)

While feeling abandoned by the Lord: "But I have trusted in your steadfast love . . ." (Psalm 13:5)

While being betrayed by his closest friend: "But you, O Lord, be gracious to me . . ." (Psalm 41:10)

Each time, while experiencing trouble in the world,

David made this choice. And I thought, there has to be something to this. If it shows up this much throughout Scripture, God has got to be asking us to take notice.

Over time, I deliberately chose to believe God was for me, even though it didn't feel like it. And as I did that, my situation may have remained the same, but my outlook didn't.

For example, I chose to believe that God was the ultimate provider of justice. This didn't mean I was going to roll over and let it all go. It meant I could rest, knowing God

SLOWLY, I CHOSE TO BELIEVE GOD WAS FOR ME, EVEN IF IT DIDN'T FEEL LIKE IT.

will do what's best, although not necessarily what I want.

I chose to believe that God is my comforter. This doesn't mean I stopped hurting. Instead I saw purpose in my pain, knowing he was close to the brokenhearted and comforted me in my affliction.

There are countless ways we can choose to believe God in our own circumstances, countless ways to shift our focus from earthly hurt to our heavenly Father. But how do we do that? What does it actually look like to make these choices day in and day out? We're going to explore these questions together.

05 | CHOOSING JOY OR CHOOSING BELIEF

While I walked through grief, healing, processing, and loss, well-meaning people told me these things:

> God works all things together for your good.
> At least it's not as bad as (fill in the blank).
> It could be worse.
> Just take your thoughts captive.
> Becky, you should just choose joy.

And listen, these are not untrue things; they're just *unhelpful*—especially in a time of much suffering. And while reading through the Psalms, a joyful attitude is not what I see from David at all. Instead, I see David settling into joy as a result of choosing God and that's a big difference.

The positive sentiments we often spew without a second thought, while rooted in Scripture, are trying to shift an *attitude* instead of your entire focus. It's like trying to curb a child's behavior without trying to curb a child's heart.

Take my thirteen-year-old, for example. A few years ago, he lied to us a lot. I'm not talking lying here and there about whether he took a cookie without asking. I'm talking about big lies that indicated a much larger problem coming from his heart.

After we discovered one of these lies, I walked through Target with a heavy spirit. I kept praying, "Lord, what else is going on here?" We could punish him all day long—take away video games, make him write out Scriptures on dishonesty, confine him to his room. But at the end of the day, there was something going on internally that we, as parents, could not seem to get at.

Similarly, when we tell each other—or even ourselves—that we should get over our heartache and choose joy already, we are failing to address the issues going on in our hearts. For twenty years I tried to be joyful while shoving my heartache down and not addressing it with the Lord.

TO BE HONEST, I NEVER COULD QUITE GET TO THE JOY PART.

To be honest, I never could quite get to the joy part. I would get so close I could taste it, and I got good at pretending—extremely good, actually. But, after digging into this idea of

The Pivot, I have found it is nearly impossible to "choose joy" without first choosing belief.

"Rejoice in the Lord always; again I will say, rejoice." (Philippians 4:4)

When I first met Jeff, this was his "life verse." He wrote it on everything, every note scribbled across a torn sheet of paper, every card, every yearbook signature. He even told me once he wanted a license plate for his '86 blue Blazer that read PHIL 4 4.

Recently I asked Jeff why this was his favorite verse for so long and his immediate response was, "Because it's emphatic." As if, Paul had no other option than to throw himself all in to praise the Lord.

Ironically, Paul, the man who penned this verse, is the same man who was thrown into prison, beaten and ridiculed and persecuted. A self-description of his ministry includes "afflictions, hardships, calamities, beatings, imprisonments, riots, labors, sleepless nights, hunger," and yet he tells us to rejoice always. (2 Corinthians 6:4-5)

So what does this mean for you and me?

It means that joy is not what overcomes us in the absence of hardship; in fact it's likely the exact opposite. A few sentences after describing the hardship of ministry, Paul continues to the Corinthians, "In all our affliction, I am *overflowing with joy*." (2 Corinthians 7:4, emphasis mine)

He's telling us that we can not only find joy in the present trials of life, but we can find joy *because of* those very trials.

In my experience, seasons of hardship have brought me closer to God. When I am comfortable, I put off seeking the Lord, put off prayer and Bible study. Maybe it's because I subconsciously think I don't need him as much. Maybe there comes a point in my comfort that I think, "I've got this; stand back, God. Watch me work."

IT'S NEARLY IMPOSSIBLE TO CHOOSE JOY WITHOUT FIRST CHOOSING BELIEF.

But when the season of comfort turns to a season of conflict—oh my goodness—my attitude shifts. And as my attitude shifts back to Jesus, so does my heart. No matter comfort or conflict, when my heart believes God to be the God he says that he is, joy is the result.

In the book of John, Jesus commands those who believe in him to abide in him. The Hebrew word for abide is ménō.[1] One translation for this word, is "remain;" another is "to be held, kept continually."

I love the idea of being kept continually by Jesus. And there is a reason we should want to.

When Jesus gives the command to abide, he and his disciples are sharing in the last supper together. He knows what is about to happen while the disciples are most likely gathered in confusion. Jesus talks cryptically about Peter denying him and Judas betraying him, but then soon after he adds, "'I am the true vine, and my Father is the vinedresser.'" (John 15:1)

I can imagine his disciples looking at each other thinking, "What does that even mean?"

Jesus is giving them (and us) a beautiful picture of being the main life-source. We are merely branches that come from it. He says, "'Abide in me, and I in you. As the branch cannot bear fruit by itself, unless it abides in the vine, neither can you, unless you abide in me.'" (John 15:4)

He's emphasizing, "Be held by me. Be kept continually by me. Remain in me."

Jesus goes on to further explain, "'I am the vine, you are the branches. Whoever abides in me and I in him, he it is that bears much fruit, for apart from me you can do nothing.'" (John 15:5)

Unless we abide in Jesus—unless we remain continually attached to him— we can literally do nothing. Jesus is telling us to stick close, know him, trust him, and believe in him by abiding in him—the vine. Then, and only then, will we be able to bear any sort of fruit—including joy.

And in this case, we have to *work* to stay connected to the vine, it doesn't just happen. We know that a branch cannot stay alive without being attached to the vine, never mind be able to bear fruit.

But Jesus is telling us that even when we cannot see a glimpse of a fruit blossom, we are supposed to keep going, keep meeting, keep praying, keep remaining attached to him. No matter what we see, how we feel, or what the current season is like. Repeatedly in Scripture Jesus addresses this by telling us we will have hardship—there will be winter seasons. We should expect it.

James 1:2 tells us to "count it all joy" when we encounter various trials. I don't know about you, but this seems nearly impossible at times. But the takeaway here is that we don't have to pretend like everything's perfect and we're always happy. We don't need to force joy or get frustrated when it doesn't come. We don't need to pretend that we don't feel pain or that life is only cupcakes and unicorns. Scripture says this is not the life of a believer.

BELIEF IS NOT THE RESULT OF CHOOSING JOY. JOY IS THE RESULT OF CHOOSING BELIEF.

Jesus so beautifully follows up his analogy of the vine with this powerful statement: "These things I have spoken to you, that my joy may be in you, and that your joy may be full." (John 15:11)

Our joy is made full in bearing fruit. Fruit-bearing is made possible by abiding in Jesus. Abiding in Jesus means living the life of a believer, with him and for him. But we now also know that in that life, the life of the believer, we *will* have trouble.

I'm going to say something that I think might be controversial: Belief is not the result of choosing joy. Joy is the result of choosing belief.

So maybe, if we aren't experiencing joy in our lives, we should be asking ourselves only one question: What am I *not* believing about God?

Perhaps your lack of joy is coming from a belief that God isn't, in fact, good. Maybe you're doubting his plans for your life or if you even have a purpose. Maybe you're wondering how God could love someone like you with all you've done.

I want to encourage you in this moment to bring your doubt back to God's Word and choose to believe him; joy will follow your belief.

Maybe it's easy for you to "choose joy" so you haven't had to give this much thought before. Maybe you're a glass half-full person, and it comes more naturally to you than focusing on the difficult things in life. And if that's you, well, friend, I am genuinely excited for you.

> **WHEN IT COMES DOWN TO IT, MAYBE WE JUST DON'T BELIEVE HIM.**

But for those of us who struggle with the feeling joyful part—those of us who have been wondering all their life, "why can't I just stinkin' have joy today"—maybe it's not because we aren't choosing joy but because we aren't believing God.

Sure, we love him. We believe *in* him. We want to serve

him. But when it comes down to it, maybe we just don't believe him.

We've gone through the motions, sang the worship songs, prayed the prayers, and finished the Bible studies. We've attended church camps and gone on mission trips and volunteered for VBS. But we still can't find it. We can't find the joy deep down in our hearts.

For twenty years I tried to choose joy without choosing belief. I had a relationship with the Lord, I loved him, I served him. I did everything right, I followed all the rules and girl, I really wanted Jesus. For. *Real.* But by keeping my secret hidden for all those years, I chose to believe God was for everyone else, but not for me.

His peace was for the girl who didn't have trauma in her background.

His purposes were for the girl who knew where her life was headed.

His forgiveness was reserved for the girl who said no and walked away.

His sovereignty was for the girl who hadn't lost a baby, who had a father who truly loved her.

I believed *in* God but didn't believe God. I believed he loved me, but only parts of me. I believed God loved me enough to save me from an eternity in hell, but not enough to save me from hell on earth.

YOU WILL SEEK ME & FIND ME, WHEN YOU SEEK ME WITH ALL YOUR HEART.

jeremiah 29:13

06 | A BLUEPRINT FOR BELIEF

Sometimes believing God comes easy because you see miracles happening. He feels near to you, feeding you manna and leading by smoke and fire.

But other times—most times, even—we're just gonna have to choose it. Over and over again. That's the hard thing about faith, though. Believing without understanding, trusting without feeling, moving forward without seeing.

If you're anything like me, you read books like this and think, "That's all well and good for *you*, but that's not going to work for me." So what does this actually look like?

I wish I could give you a "how to" or a step-by-step guide to throwing off your doubt and believing in God. But unfortunately, no one can control your thoughts except you. No one can make you believe, and if God doesn't force you to do it, I certainly can't.

But I *can* share with what I've experienced over the last several years that has challenged me to take God at his word every single time—even when it's difficult and especially when I really, really didn't want to.

1. KNOW GOD

We can't believe God is all he says he is if we don't *know* who he says he is. (You might need to read that one again.) You can't know what Scripture teaches without first reading Scripture.

I became a believer at a very young age—probably six or seven—while memorizing the twenty-third Psalm. There was something about the Lord being my shepherd that spoke to the deepest part of me, even as a small child. Maybe I knew that in the long run, I would need a caretaker who wasn't flawed like my people on earth. Maybe God chose to etch that moment in my brain forever to remind me of his character in the darkest valley.

Whatever the reason, it was my moment.

I have a friend who grew up in church and loved Jesus. She served and prayed and worshiped. She went to youth camps and mission trips. After graduating college and getting married, she attended a Sunday School class, the class that we would eventually meet in and become forever friends. But during that season, she realized she never had a relationship with Jesus. She had served and loved him, yes, but never known him, personally.

So she had her moment.

It was nothing special or magical, but it was *hers*. The moment when she asked the Lord to be the savior of her life, forever.

Have you had your own moment with Jesus?

You can believe God is real, believe he is love, believe he is a miracle worker, all while not having a relationship with him.

Think about it like this, I

HAVE YOU HAD YOUR OWN MOMENT WITH JESUS?

know many people in my neighborhood. Women I might meet a time or two at a PTA meeting or a book fair. They have kids my kids' ages or walk their dog in front of my house while I'm watering my flowers. They're nice, I know their names, and I might even know where they live.

But I don't know them. I don't know their hurts, their background, their hearts. I don't know their struggles, their beliefs, their passions.

Do you know Jesus?

It's not complicated or weird or awkward to have a relationship with Jesus.

It's as simple as admitting to God that you're a sinner and you will never be perfect. It's acknowledging that God is perfect and therefore requires our perfection. And thankfully, since we created a gap between his perfection and our humanity, he gave us Jesus to fill it in. A relationship with Jesus begins by believing that he died on the cross for us—for you—so that you can enter a relationship with God, being made perfect not by anything you've done, but by Jesus's perfect blood.

We cannot even begin to believe God without knowing God.

2. STUDY THE WORD OF GOD

Several years ago, way back before I decided to give Jesus my broken pieces along with the good parts, I felt dry like I never had before. I was praying and attending Bible study and going through the right motions. I was being discipled by a woman I adored in the church, serving the church, and reading all the books about living a life of faith.

But I still felt alone. It was as if all my prayers, my cries out to the Lord, felt like they were hitting the ceiling. Was anyone even on the other side? My faith became stagnant and still. I stopped growing spiritually, even though I was taking in all sorts of information.

I confided in my mentor that not only was I not feeling like myself, but I felt like God had left me. Even though I knew God doesn't abandon his children, I couldn't help how I was feeling.

She asked me, "How are you spending time with God?"

I didn't even take a breath but responded with all the books I was reading and the journaling I was doing. I described how much time I was spending trying to reach

God. She listened intently and understood I was spinning my wheels. And then her piece of advice changed my life.

"Well, it seems like you're reading a lot of what other people are telling you about God, but are you reading what God says about himself?"

All the podcasts, lessons from wonderful Bible teachers, books written about God were all another human's interpretation about him. The content I was taking in was thick with theology and truth. But, it wasn't the Bible.

I left that conversation asking myself if I was spending more time reading other people's words about God instead of reading God's Word.

And I definitely was.

How was I supposed to know what I believe about God if I only knew what other people said about God? How was I supposed to have (and value) my own experiences with God's faithfulness and perfect love if I'm constantly comparing it with the experience of the person whose words I'm reading?

Books *about* God are wonderful, and of course here I am writing one! But they are not and never will be God's Word. They will never sufficiently replace Scripture. I knew I wanted to read the Bible from beginning to end to know not only the New Testament Jesus, but to know God the Father, the creator and author of the universe. And with that, what the creator of the universe says about me.

But studying the Bible felt overwhelming. Even though I took Old Testament and New Testament in college, I regrettably don't remember a thing from it. Plus, I didn't know how to study theology, I wasn't a scholar, and I was never even a good student. I tried reading the Bible in a year and gave it my best try several times. But by mid-January, I would lose my ever-loving mind with twenty chapters of genealogy and laws in Leviticus.

So I decided to start a different way.

One chapter a day, starting in Genesis 1. I didn't journal it or follow a book, but opened my Bible and read it word for word. Often twice, sometimes three times. My only goal was to learn something about God each day, which I did . . . most days, anyway.

If you know me at all, you've probably heard me say, "You're not the boss of me." I like to say it to my to-do lists, my calendar, my exercise program, and sometimes my husband. And it honestly came from my short and sweet plan to dig into the Bible. I didn't limit myself, I didn't rush, I didn't check it off a list. I not only gave myself grace, but I learned how to trust the Holy Spirit's leading in my study.

If I came across something that I didn't understand or didn't like, I would dig in a bit more. Eventually, as I became more comfortable with the freedom of reading God's Word on my own with the Holy Spirit, I would pick apart chapters for weeks to understand its richness.

You'll find many of those passages woven throughout these pages. God breathed new life into my weary and dry bones through the simple reading of His Word. The lessons I learned about God during those years gave me the strength to withstand the heartache of losing a relationship with my dad and our family as we knew it.

It was knowing who God said he was, not who Beth or Jennie or Lysa taught me he was, that challenged my faith in a new way and gave me the tools I needed to combat the enemy's attack on our lives.

3. DEVELOP A PRAYER LIFE

Do you talk to yourself?

I talk to myself all the time, and when I say all the time, I mean *all* the time. I'm so glad we don't have cameras inside of our house because Jeff would be able to drop in and hear me having full-on conversations all day long . . . with myself.

I'm an external processor, so most of my conversations revolve around what I *should* have said, what I *want* to say, or what I can't believe someone else said yesterday. It's often either preempting a situation or rehashing one I wish had gone differently.

But recently over coffee, a friend recounted teaching a lesson on prayer. Her point was that prayer doesn't have to be anything fancy; it can be a constant conversation with the Lord. She told me she prayed out loud in the car on the way to our coffee, while she does the dishes, while she cleans up her house. She prays about everything.

"I talk to myself about everything," I said to her that day. We almost died laughing because, it's funny. But it also made me sad.

I *never* prayed. Well, I rarely prayed beyond the whole

"God, could you help me in this situation" thing. After I left coffee, I got in my car with this idea rolling around in my head when I flipped on a podcast by another friend talking about the same thing— praying without ceasing.

This is what I like to call a "Holy Echo," and God was getting my attention.

While I'm in a deep and consistent habit of reading Scripture, I hated to admit that I'm not in a habit of praying. I might utter a word or two in the morning or evening and especially before mealtime to "bless" the food. But I lacked an invigorating prayer life.

So I decided to change things up.

Instead of talking to myself, I talked to God. Aloud. Every single time I heard myself having a conversation alone, I switched my audience to the Lord. So if I was rehashing a situation, instead of going around in circles about what I wish would have gone differently, I prayed about it. I asked the Lord to bless the person I was upset with, ask him to show me my own shortcomings, ask for forgiveness for my often bitter heart. I would tell him about my hurt feelings, my disappointment, my anger. I would tell him how insecure or alone I felt, how upset I was, and ask him to help. To lead. To just make me feel his presence.

And you know what happened?

> **INSTEAD OF TALKING TO MYSELF, I TALKED TO GOD.**

He showed up.

It was crazy. There were times I prayed for God to prioritize my day, and he would bring a specific person to my mind. I would reach out and encourage, and often receive a text back saying, "You have no idea how timely this was." He gave us opportunities for spiritual conversations with waiters or waitresses. He would provide sources of encouragement in ways I had never experienced before.

There is something that happens when we pray and God answers—it solidifies our faith.

In Luke 18, Jesus tells a parable about a persistent widow seeking justice. She pestered the judge who didn't know God and didn't respect any man in order that she might find justice against her enemy. Finally, after much persistence from the woman, he granted her the justice she wanted.

Then Jesus said, "'And will not God give justice to his elect, who cry to him day and night? Will he delay long over them?'" (Luke 18:7)

Cry to him day and night. Tell him your heartache and your hurt. Let him in on the struggles of your soul, the anxiety and depression you are feeling. Let him heal you, give you peace, encouragement, conviction of sin even.

And when he does this, your faith, and your capacity to believe him, will deepen.

4. PRACTICE BELIEF

After a year of healing from my abuse, I shared my story publicly for the first time. I was at my church in a women's conference—the church I grew up in. The church my father taught Sunday school and sang in the choir. The church my husband was literally born into, and my mom taught Bible study and VBS.

And here I was on a stage in front of three hundred women about to reveal my deepest shame hoping it would help someone else share theirs.

My goal was never, and never will be, to shame my father for the awful choices he made. My goal was, and always will be, to testify of what God has brought me through. The abuse, of course, but also the fall out. Grieving the relationship with my father, begging for reconciliation that never came, transforming my thoughts of shame.

And as I began to share more publicly about my story and God's story written in me, I also began hearing from others with similar backgrounds. I still receive messages from women consistently, and occasionally from some men. I get questions like, "How could a good God allow this to happen to me" and "Was God watching when we were abused?"

All difficult, but good questions. Questions, to be honest, that are "above my pay grade."

And as I try to work it out with them, speaking from a place of sincere understanding and never ever from a place of judgment, I eventually get to this point with each of them.

Even in your wrestling with the Lord's ways and trying

to understand these difficult things—like why do bad things happen to "good" people—at the end of the day, you have a choice to make. Are you going to run to God or from God?

Are you going to believe him or not?

There are certainly many days that I don't. I sit on my couch with my mom or husband and say, "This isn't fair" and "How could God be so mean?" But eventually, I pivot from my doubt, my hurt, my fear, and legit practice belief.

It's a discipline that won't come easy at first, but the more you know God, know his Word, and pray, the easier it becomes.

BELIEF IS A DAILY DISCIPLINE, NOT A ONE-TIME DECISION.

The more you see and experience his hand at work in your life, the more you will be naturally inclined to choose belief.

But it starts as a practice. Belief is a daily discipline, not a one-time decision. It's an internal day-by-day choice to believe God. To believe that he's who he says he is and believe that you are who he says you are. It's choosing to believe that his purposes and plans for you are *good*, that he is your friend and will never leave you. It's a choice to believe that he is a faithful God, full of grace, forgiveness, justice, and mercy all at the same time. And yes, it's a choice you will forever make.

You might not *feel* like doing it, and sometimes it will feel easier to be sad, angry, resentful, lonely. But each time you make the choice to believe, your faith will grow deeper, your experience with God will grow wider, and your joy will become clearer.

The next pages are full of difficult times I made that choice, and even times I didn't. I'll tell stories of deep heartache and loss, but also stories of flat-out falling on my face. Stories of broken relationships, times God provided healing and times he didn't. But I don't want you to take my word for it. I want these stories to encourage you to dive deep into Scripture. I want you to see how to lean into his promises, read them for yourself and know, without a shadow of a doubt, that God is good to you.

> **CHOOSING BELIEF IS ONE OF THE HARDEST LESSONS I'VE LEARNED, BUT I NEVER REGRET MAKING THAT CHOICE.**

In every chapter, I will relate my circumstances back to a story, a person, a promise I've seen in the Bible. I find comfort in knowing I'm not the only one who has felt unseen, unloved, or unworthy, and I hope you will too. After reading Scripture, knowing that God does in fact see me, love me, and find value in me is the best gift I could ever receive. And my hope in sharing the good, the bad, and the ugly will make you feel grateful for God's gift to you too.

Choosing belief is one of the hardest lessons I've learned, but I never regret making that choice. I've never believed something about God and then come back and said, "Man, I wish I had doubted him here." I've never lived through a struggle and realized, "Well, he really isn't as faithful as he said he would be."

God comes through every time, even when it's not in the way or speed I want him to. He provides peace and comfort, his love is steadfast, he has new mercies that are lavished on us every single morning. And I desperately want you to experience those mercies too. I want you to feel his faithfulness too.

So if you are weary, hurting, alone, or desperate, keep digging through these pages, alongside God's Word, I promise he will meet you exactly where you are every single time. You will not be disappointed.

PART TWO

GOD IS OUR REFUGE & STRENGTH, A VERY PRESENT HELP IN TROUBLE.

psalm 46:1

07 | BELIEVING GOD IS ENOUGH

when everything else is falling apart

I lost sleep many times throughout the secret-keeping years as I contemplated spilling my guts to my husband. As I ran through various scenarios in my head of how it could play out, accusation would roll in:

> How could you keep a secret from him for so long?
>
> You betrayed him.
>
> He'll never believe you.
>
> He'll never trust you again.
>
> If he does believe you, he'll leave you.
>
> He could never look at you the same after this.
>
> You're disgusting. This is your fault. You're an awful

wife, daughter, and mom.

Have you ever been in this situation—accusations swimming to the edges of your mind? These thoughts held me captive for most of my life. These thoughts were the main reason I stayed silent for all those years.

But these thoughts, I would soon realize, were not from the Lord.

Days after speaking my secret aloud for the first time to a stranger, Jeff and I sat down on the couch to watch a television show. The kids were tucked into bed and the house was quiet. My face was washed, pajamas on, and tea poured.

Like so many moms, this is my very favorite time of day.

But in this moment, on this night, my heart pounded loud enough I'm sure Jeff heard it. Knowing what I needed to do but not wanting to, tears silently fell as Ross and Rachel bantered on the screen. I kept very still, making sure to face forward, hoping Jeff wouldn't notice but mostly hoping he wouldn't ask any questions.

Hoping I could put it off for just one more day.

Jeff grabbed my hand, switched the television off, turned to face me, and gently said, "Tell me."

How could I even start?

I don't remember any of the words that came out of my mouth other than, "I am so sorry, Jeff. I am just so, so sorry." As I talked and told the story bit by bit, putting words to what is nearly impossible to put words to, he sat and listened, never letting my hands go. After I finished, he took a deep breath and calmly asked a handful of questions, being careful not to press me too hard.

I answered what I could, or rather, what I *would* answer, then waited for his reaction. I flinched with every move he made thinking, *This is it—this is when he packs his bags and he leaves.* Convincing yourself you're guilty when you're not for any amount of time will wreak havoc on your self-esteem, let me tell ya. And because of that, I was halfway expecting Jeff to get up and walk out that door.

Please hear me when I tell you that thinking he would leave had nothing to do with him, and everything to do with the whispers in my head and the years of berating myself for what I should have done and not done.

But much to my surprise, and my relief, he didn't leave. He stayed.

Things were different for sure.

I became a quieter, toned-down version of myself, positive he was judging me, even while promising the opposite.

Jeff quieted as well. After knowing me for twenty years, processing the bomb I had just dropped must have been difficult. I couldn't possibly comprehend what was going through his mind.

We'd been dating while much of my abuse happened, the especially gross parts of it actually. His continued heartbreak was not only that it happened, but that he didn't save me from it . . . that he didn't even know I needed saving.

A few days later, while sitting outside for dinner, we watched our youngest run around the yard like a crazy person. He chased our sweet elderly dog back and forth while laughing his cute little head off. My heart felt heavy at the quiet tension between us, but I smiled anyway.

Then Jeff said, without looking at me, "I have a confession."

Here it comes, I thought.

He took a deep breath, still staring away, and said, "Look, Becky, I'm really angry. Like, *really* angry."

The air was cooling from an unseasonably warm January day. The sky darkened enough so I could hide my tears. Again, my body tensed, I shut my eyes, and I squeezed out a shaky response. "I understand. I just can't say I'm sorry enough."

He shot up and came over to me. He got down on my level and stooped right in front of my face, softly but firmly gripping my shoulders.

"Becky Leach, listen to me. I am not mad at you. I need you to understand that. I'm not mad at you. I'm not mad at you. I'm not mad at you." He took a breath. "But I'm really mad at your dad."

I sobbed as twenty years' worth of shame and grief poured out. I felt a tidal wave of relief and held onto my husband, my rock, for dear life.

To know someone could not only love me while knowing my deepest, darkest secret, but also want to fight with and for me, changed the course of my life.

Because unfortunately for me, the next several months would be a lot like this. Bracing for a storm without knowing what was on the other side.

But for the first time, maybe in my entire life, I felt free.

Here's the thing with acknowledging baggage in your life.

Whether it's something from your past or present, a sin or a circumstance, a relationship that has become toxic or a relationship that never happened, in order to surrender it all, you have to be willing to risk it all.

I knew I could end up alone. I knew I might not be believed or that I might be blamed. I knew my dad might deny it. I knew the risk of telling my secret, but I had come to a point where I was either willing to take that risk or risk a half-lived, half-truthful, and anxious life with more regrets and what if's than I could ever count.

> IN ORDER TO SURRENDER IT ALL, YOU HAVE TO BE WILLING TO RISK IT ALL.

Thank the Lord I didn't end up alone, that my family stayed by my side, supported me, and believed me. I was thankful that I even got a half-confession out of my father before our relationship disintegrated. But it might have not ended up that way, and even as it stands, we have suffered great relational loss.

Even though people stayed, not *everyone* stayed. Even though the important people believed me, not *everyone* believed me. And even though I didn't end up alone, I understood there was a risk of it happening. But I decided to take it anyway.

Maybe that's where you are too. Maybe you're on the verge of releasing something scary into the world. Or perhaps you're waiting to let go of who you were, or who you wanted to be. Maybe you've been lying to yourself, not just everyone else, and fear that if you get honest, everyone else will get honest with you too.

WHAT IF YOU CAN'T MOVE FORWARD BECAUSE YOU FIRST NEED TO LET GO?

Or maybe, just maybe, you're contemplating if it's worth the risk. You're asking yourself whether you can handle the potential change or if you could live without that person, that thing, or that dream.

If you're like me, you've been stuck at this crossroads for a long time. For as many times as I kept my mouth shut, holding it all together while holding it all in, I was one deep breath away from spilling it. But the Lord brought me to a breaking point so that I would choose to believe him.

So let me give you something to think about: what if you can't move forward because you first need to let go? What if the reason you feel stuck is because God is trying to pry your hands off something?

The decision I made wasn't just to let go of what I was hiding while letting others in. The decision was also—maybe more so—that even if I was left all alone on this earth, my God would be enough.

THE PASSAGE

Scripture is filled with stories of men, women, and even children willing to risk it all. There's the story of Abraham who was told to sacrifice the child he had waited a hundred years for. He believed God would provide another sacrifice and strapped his young boy to the altar before God intervened.

There's the story of David and Goliath, the small young kid facing a giant with just three rocks in his pocket, believing God would take care of him.

The story of Shadrach, Meshach, and Abednego who wouldn't bow down to their king, risking death.

The story of Daniel and the lion's den.

The story of Esther asking her husband, the king, for protection of her people—also risking death.

These are the brave and bold stories of people putting their lives (or their children's lives) on the line to obey the Lord, believing he was big enough to take care of it all.

But one of my favorite brave stories to read is Noah and the ark.

If you grew up in or around church, I bet you feel the

same way. This is one of the first Bible stories I learned in Sunday school. It has the best coloring pages with animals and rainbows and holds a child's attention with awe and wonder, the end of the story promising God's forever faithfulness to his people.

But as an adult when I look at it, I find it's also a very sad story.

Many years before, Adam and Eve sinned, were cast out of the garden of Eden, and started to populate the earth. People lived hundreds of years in that day—hundreds!— so Adam had his first son when he was 130 years old and lived until he was 930! Can you even imagine? I was tired having a child at thirty, much less 130!

At the start of the story, Noah was 500 years old and had fathered three sons: Shem, Ham and Japheth. But as the earth held more people, "the Lord saw that the wickedness of man was great in the earth, and that every intention of the thoughts of his heart was only evil *continually*." (Genesis 6:5, emphasis mine)

We don't know why this is specifically.

We don't know how things took a turn in a few short verses, although it spanned at least a thousand years between Adam and Noah. I get lost in questions like, What was the wickedness in their heart? What temptations did they give in to? We don't know much here. We just know that the Lord saw that every intention of man was evil. So much so that "the Lord regretted that he had made man on the earth, and it grieved him to his heart." (Genesis 6:6)

Can you even imagine grieving God in such a way that he regretted making you? Their sin must have been pretty messed up.

So then God decides to "blot out" all of mankind from the earth and start over, "but Noah found favor in the eyes of the Lord." (Genesis 6:8)

Now we're getting to the good part—the "Sunday school" part.

Yes, Noah built the ark and paid careful attention to all the Lord asked him to do. I'm impressed that he followed the specific directions God laid out for him as he built the ark, but do you ever wonder what the people around him thought? Have you ever wondered how they might have gawked and made fun of him?

We recently introduced our kids to the movie, *Evan Almighty*. It's a hilarious, and touching, movie about a dad (Steve Carell) who spends too much time away from his kids, but God (Morgan Freeman, of course) gets a hold of him and asks him to build an ark because a big flood is coming. As he builds, everyone makes fun of him. His wife and kids at first think he's gone mad. His coworkers talk about sending him to the looney bin. The news channels taunt him; his neighbors roll their eyes.

This gives a silly, but likely accurate, picture of Noah's day, God deeming every single person on the earth—outside of his family—evil. So, as I read this story, I am now overwhelmed by Noah's risky belief that God had a purpose in building this ark. He so deeply took God at his word—that a flood would indeed come—that he didn't care what anyone else said or thought about him or his family.

He must have left friendships, workplaces, even his community to obey. He must have looked like an idiot to the rest of the world, building this monstrosity for some mysterious event called a flood. He must have laid it all down to walk in obedience to the Lord.

And, to add insult to injury, he wasn't building a luxury cruise ship. It was a basic but large boat, built to house his family and at least two of each animal that existed at the time.

HE MUST HAVE LAID IT **ALL** DOWN TO WALK IN OBEDIENCE TO THE LORD.

It was a dirty, stinky, and dark ship.

At the end of the day, what if the boat sank? What if his family decided not to come? What if they didn't believe him?

When he started to build the ark, he had to decide whether he would *believe* that God would be enough when everything and everyone on the face of the earth was blotted out.

That's a big ask.

But he believed it.

THE PIVOT

Days after we confronted my parents, I knew life would never be the same for our family, for our marriage, and for our kids. For my sister and brother, niece and nephews. For my mom. We would no longer be the family we knew, and at that point I wasn't sure if it would be for the better.

In my heartache, I reached for the Psalms. As I've mentioned before, they bring much peace; I feel kinship with David as his honest emotions spill out on the page before us and the Lord.

Psalm 46 starts like this, "God is our refuge and strength, a very present help in trouble." (Psalm 46:1) The psalmist acknowledges who he knows God to be. He reminds us, but it seems he might also be reminding himself.

He continues, "Therefore we will not fear though the earth gives way, though the mountains be moved into the heart of the sea, though its waters roar and foam, though the mountains tremble at its swelling." (Psalm 46:2-3)

We need to recognize the radical nature of this threat. He's saying that even if the earth is destroyed, we should not fear. Even if a volcano or a flood threatens everything around us, we should not fear. I don't know how you deal with impending threats, but I would be a nervous wreck if the earth was about to be destroyed.

When I first studied this passage of Scripture, I read that a mountain is often used in the Bible as a metaphor for something unchangeable and immovable.

Just think about this for a second: We have seen cliffs slide into the sea. We've seen mudslides and sink holes throughout our lifetime, even if only on television. But have you ever seen a mountain *crumble* into the sea? I most certainly haven't.

We recently traveled to Colorado and took our kids to the Red Rocks Amphitheater in Morrison. If you've never been there, you should go but be prepared for an altitude adjustment and one million and forty-two steps. (That calculation might be a *slight* exaggeration.)

After much complaining from our tired and sweaty children, we made it to the top of the amphitheater, looking out to the valley on one side and the wide expanse of the Rocky Mountains on the other.

It was breathtaking and beautiful. It was powerful and majestic. And all I could think about was this passage in Psalms—even if these mountains, that seem eternally immovable, crumbled into the heart of the sea, I should not fear. Why? Because my God oversees it all. Because my God has me *and* these mountains in the palm of his hand.

And because my God is, and will continue to be, enough for me.

When I look around today, I feel like figurative mountains are crumbling all around us. Our government, our infrastructure, our health, our foreign relations. When we watch the news, it's easy to think there's nothing stable in our lives anymore. And maybe when you look around your life, you feel the same way, as if you can't count on anything or anyone.

Or perhaps you think you've got it all together because so far, you've ignored the rubble of the mountains, pretending everything and everyone is fine.

Let me ask you this—what are the mountains in your life? What are those things that you count on beyond everything else to always remain stable?

EVEN IF YOU ARE LEFT WITH ABSOLUTELY NOTHING, GOD IS ENOUGH.

Mine have been my marriage and my family.

I stood convinced that regardless of what happened in the world, these would always stay the same. So, when faced with the decision to believe God, walk forward in honesty and obedience, while simultaneously risking that the mountain might crumble? You better believe I was scared to death. I walked with trepidation, anticipating the worst.

But at the end of the day, I did walk forward.

I had to decide that I counted on God more than I counted on that strong and stable mountain. I had to decide that even if it crumbled into a raging sea, God would never leave me. He would be enough.

Even if you are left with absolutely nothing, God is enough.

Even if everyone in your world leaves, God is enough.

Even if the surest thing in your life becomes unsure, God will always be enough.

What do you need to lay down in your life? What, *or who*, are you relying on more than the Lord? Is it wealth? Is it a relationship? Is it a career?

Whatever that mountain, are you willing to risk it crumbling for you to live an honest, raw, and beautiful life with the Lord? A life that is full of grace and freedom, one where you don't have to pretend to be perfect, one where you come to Jesus again and again in your imperfection.

> **OUR BELIEF THAT GOD IS EVERYTHING AND THE ONLY THING WILL INFORM EVERY DECISION FROM THIS MOMENT FORWARD.**

The risk is not a feeling, but a choice. It's a choice to believe—the foundational choice to believe, actually—that he is all we need. For survival, approval, love, provision. This is the choice we must make, moving from what the world tells us we should fear to the foundation of our faith. God is all we need.

Our belief that God is everything and the only thing will

inform every decision we make from this moment forward. This belief will determine whether we obey when he calls us. It will determine whether we keep secrets from God or others. It will determine whether we walk in the light or the darkness.

He is and will always be enough. For you just as he was for me. Now the question is: Will you choose to believe that?

AND WE KNOW THAT FOR THOSE WHO LOVE GOD ALL THINGS WORK TOGETHER FOR GOOD

romans 8:28

08 | **BELIEVING GOD'S PURPOSES ARE GOOD**
despite what you see in front of you

When I first revealed my abuse to my counselor and my husband, I thought the hard part was over. I told myself, "Now I don't have to tell anybody else. Now I can just work through it like a 'normal' person would."

But a week or two after my revelation, a different reality knocked on my door.

I put our two-year old son, Landry, down for a nap and heard a knock at my door. I peeked out the window and didn't recognize the woman or the car, so I let it go. But she continued to knock, then bang. I went back downstairs, concerned at her insistence.

Then my phone rang.

Let me back up for a second. On my second counseling visit, my sweet therapist informed me that she had to report my case to CPS because my father still "had access" to children (my children, specifically). Sitting on that couch, I was beside myself—angry, even. I had trusted her.

She understood my feelings but assured me it would be no big deal. Because the abuse happened twenty years ago and CPS had no other information, they would probably call me and ask a few questions and that would be that. Fine.

So the next day when an unknown number popped up on my phone after this insistent knocking, I thought, this must be CPS. I answered.

What happened next still makes me anxious.

"This is Becky." (I aways answer unknown numbers like this to sound incredibly professional.)

"Hi, Ms. Leach. This is Child Protective Services, and I need to make an appointment to speak to you, your husband, and your other child."

"An appointment? Can we just speak on the phone?"

"No ma'am. I need to speak with each of you individually and in person."

"Wait a minute. What do you mean my *other* child? I have three children."

"Right. I've already spoken to your older children, and they did not make an outcry. But I need to speak with your youngest child."

The world halted. My heart stopped. I felt like I would vomit in my kitchen sink. What. Was. Happening.

"Excuse me? You've already spoken to my children? Where did you speak to my children? I didn't give you permission to speak to them. They have no idea what it is going on. How dare you bring them into this."

I was devastated with a million thoughts running through my head.

No one was *ever* supposed to know about this. And now, not only did they know, but since we go to a small public elementary school within our community, our *entire* neighborhood knew. And our teachers that we loved so much. And our children.

My mind spun.

What do they think? What do they know? What did she tell them?

I was embarrassed, ashamed, scared, and angry.

But what I didn't know then, but know now three years later, is that God had ordained this moment for so many reasons. He knew I would need assurance that

SOMETIMES GOD HAS TO BREAK IT ALL DOWN TO BUILD IT BACK UP.

my father didn't harm our children. He knew that interview would bring my siblings in and create the first step to confront my secret abuse.

Did it feel good? Absolutely not. Thinking about it even still makes my stomach sick. But sometimes God has to break it all down to build it back up.

THE PASSAGE

Maybe you're in a similar situation—not that CPS unexpectedly came out to interview your kids—but that something unfair is breaking you apart. Perhaps you're wondering where God is and if he could possibly take all that is broken and do something good. I want to come alongside of you today and whisper, "You are not alone."

We are in good company, my friends. Let's look at Ruth, Naomi, and Orpah, shall we?

When the book of Ruth begins, the land of Judah is experiencing famine. So a man named Elimelech and his wife Naomi left Judah with their two sons and traveled to Moab. It's not specific, but my assumption is Moab was not experiencing the same famine.

Moab was a pagan land. In fact, the Moabites were born out of incest between Lot and one of his daughters, after the destruction of Sodom and Gomorrah. (Genesis 19:37–38) According to the Encyclopedia Britannica, the Moabites worshiped Chemosh, an ancient West Semitic deity.[1]

So we first meet Ruth after her father-in-law dies. Naomi, her mother-in-law, stays with her family, her brother, and sister-in-law in Moab. Then ten years later, both of Naomi's sons die—Ruth's husband and Orpah's husband.

Naomi travels back with the girls to her home of Judah because a few relatives could care for them there. But on their journey, Naomi famously tells both of her daughters-in-law to stay in Moab because she has nothing to offer either one of them in terms of marriage, money, or land.

Naomi must have been one heck of a mother-in-law, because both Orpah and Ruth wept at the thought of leaving her and promised to stay by her side. Orpah eventually decides to stay behind, but Scripture says that "Ruth clung to her." (Ruth 1:14)

> Naomi starts, "'See, your sister-in-law has gone back to her people and to her gods; return after your sister-in law.' But Ruth said, 'Do not urge me to live you or to return from following you. For where you go I will go, and where you lodge I will lodge. Your people shall be my people, and your God my God. Where you die I will die, and there will I be buried. May the Lord do so to me and more also if anything but death parts me from you.' And when Naomi saw that she was determined to go with her, she said no more." (Ruth 1:15-18)

Now, *that's* some devotion.

While most of the book of Ruth focuses on Ruth, I want to shift our focus back to Naomi.

She has suffered much. She experienced famine, lost her husband and both of her sons, potentially at the same time. She journeyed back to her home of Judah with nothing, so incredibly grief-stricken that she tells her friends, "'Do not call me Naomi; call me Mara, for the Almighty has dealt very bitterly with me.'" (Ruth 1:20)

The text doesn't explicitly tell us this, but if we look closely, we can assume she must have suffered well. We know because both of her daughters-in-law wanted to follow her back to her land. I don't know what your relationship with your mother-in-law is like, but I would say that is a rare occurrence, wouldn't you? They weren't trying to find the first way out; they were going above and beyond their duty as "family" to this woman whom they loved so dearly.

> **NAOMI'S SUFFERING REVEALED HER FAITH. HER GRIEF POINTED TO HER BELIEF IN GOD.**

Could it be that Naomi's suffering revealed her faith? Could it be her inexplicable grief pointed to her belief in God and his faithfulness each step of the way?

This didn't mean she wasn't sad—we *know* she was sad, bitter even. But when I read between the lines, what I see is a woman who knew that despite her situation, God was faithful. He would continue to provide.

I can only imagine the profound impact on both women, but we see it especially in Ruth. Remember, she likely served a pagan god as a Moabite woman, but instead, she tells Naomi that her God would now be her own God.

God's purposes, albeit difficult for Naomi and Ruth, were, in the end, good. Can you see it?

THE PIVOT

What circumstances in your life seem difficult but just might, in the end, be good?

When I dove into writing this book, I promised myself to not use this verse in Romans because people tried to slap it on my gaping wound like a Band-Aid. They would say it to "make me feel better," but what I took from it was a "hurry up and get over it so I don't have to listen to this anymore" kind of vibe.

But in all honesty, this verse is one of the most profound and pivotal truths we find in Scripture. I am going to write it out in the Message translation because it explains it so clearly for us.

> Meanwhile, the moment we get tired in the waiting, God's Spirit is right alongside helping us along. If we don't know how or what to pray, it doesn't matter. He does our praying in and for us, making prayer out of our wordless sighs, our aching groans. He knows us far better than we know ourselves, knows our pregnant condition, and keeps us present before God. That's why we can be so sure that every detail in our lives of love for God is worked into something good. (Romans 8:26-28, MSG)

Every detail in our lives is worked into something good. Do you believe it?

Do you believe that the hard and difficult seasons you are experiencing or have experienced can and will work into something good?

Sometimes I get tired of waiting. Right now, even, I am tired of waiting to see the something good. I can see glimpses of it, but all in all, some parts of my life feel unfair, and the good I want to see I'm almost positive I'll never see.

"I WILL BELIEVE THAT GOD CAN AND WILL DO IT BECAUSE I'VE SEEN HIM DO IT BEFORE.

But I will believe. I will believe that God can and will do it, because I've seen him do it before. I've read about him doing it for the Israelites, I've heard testimonies about him doing it for my friends, and I've experienced it in my own life. And if he's done it before, I have to believe that he will do it again.

Will I see it? Maybe. But if I don't, I will still choose to believe.

We have to pivot from what we see happening in front of us to what we know will happen with the Lord in charge. We must know in the deepest parts of our heart that his plans and purposes for us are good—even if we don't ever understand them this side of heaven. In our devastation, we can absolutely trust that God's purposes are good because he has proved it repeatedly throughout history.

The day I got the CPS call, I was broken and questioned everything I knew about God. I was angry at him. I curled up in a ball on my kitchen floor and cried my eyes out. I asked him where he was and why he allowed my heart to break again and again. Wasn't he for me? Didn't he have a plan and all I had to do was walk in it?

If you're there today, in the heartbreak, you aren't alone. And no, God did not leave you. My prayer is that you would find a way to believe his purposes are good, even if you can't see them right now. My prayer is for healing, comfort, and peace.

FOR THE SAKE OF CHRIST, THEN, I AM CONTENT WITH WEAKNESSES, INSULTS, HARDSHIPS, PERSECUTIONS, & CALAMITIES. FOR WHEN I AM WEAK, THEN I AM STRONG.

2 corinthians 12:10

09 | BELIEVING GOD IS YOUR STRENGTH
when you feel weak

A few weeks after the CPS call, I reluctantly found myself at a group workout. Now first I need to let you know that working out—especially in group settings—is not my jam. I get embarrassed when I can't keep up, can't do as many push ups as the other people. I don't like feeling everyone is looking at me, watching me fail, even if they probably aren't.

So when I say I *found* myself at this workout, it's not because I wanted to be there, but because one of our friends was leading it while training adaptive athletes. These are men and women, most of whom have lost arms or legs, doing extreme workouts. I remember our friend Shawn telling me, "If they can do it, you have no excuse," to which I rolled my eyes and sighed, unfortunately, rather loudly.

The premise of the group workout was this: in teams of 4-5 people, we would cycle through stations for an hour (yes, an entire hour). We would keep track of how many rounds we did collectively and compete against the other teams. We couldn't move on until we all did it, you get my drift?

So it mattered whether or not I could complete something, which would not be a huge deal if it weren't for the six-foot wall looming in the corner. All five foot nothing of my little self was sweating bullets at the idea of climbing that thing. And when we got there, I needed help getting up and over it each time.

After the hour was completed and we all celebrated (because our team did not lose), Jeff pointed over to the wall and said, "You can do that."

"Uh, no. The workout is over, remember?"

He shook his head, squeezed my arm firmly, and patted me on the tush like a football coach. "You're going to regret it if you don't at least try."

I rolled my eyes and took turns glaring at him and then the wall. I knew he was right, but he knew he was right too, which I hated.

Tightening up my ponytail, I walked over to it while no one was watching. I took a deep breath and a running start, but my foot slipped on the minuscule bottom ledge before I could even grab the top. The first attempt was a big fat fail. As was the second and the third.

But eventually I got one leg hooked up over the top while my right tippy toe anchored on that same ledge. I sat in that position for a while, catching my breath, before hurling myself onto the other side.

I did it.

I didn't want to, I didn't even think it was possible, but I did it.

And that lesson reminded me of so much more than climbing over a stinkin' ridiculous wall (that gave me horrible bruises for days). It reminded me that I can do hard things, not just when I want to or when it's convenient or even when I have a team of people cheering me on.

And so can you.

Now, look, I wish there was this big spiritual moment during the whole wall debacle where I asked God to supernaturally hoist me up over the wall, but there wasn't. It was pure determination (after much peer pressure) to at least try.

And sometimes that's

SOMETIMES GOD SURROUNDS US WITH PEOPLE WHO ENCOURAGE US TO DO THE HARD THING.

what God gives us. Sometimes God surrounds us with people who encourage us to try the hard thing. He gives us community who say they've got our back and to bring us meals. Sometimes God girds us with human versions of spiritual encouragement, praying over us and with us, making us laugh when we need it and pushing our hair back when we cry.

But other times we look at the wall in front of us, whether it be real or imagined, and walk the other way because it's too difficult to even think about climbing over it.

For years the wall in my life was my abuse. I couldn't bear to think about what the other side of that wall looked like, much less all the effort to climb over it.

Maybe your wall is a relationship you need to mend or a career change you need to make. Maybe you have a decision on the horizon that you don't want to make, a sin you need to confess, or a diagnosis with a treatment plan that feels impossible.

No matter what the wall is, no matter how high or difficult or even unpleasant, you don't have to figure it out on your own. You don't have to muster up the strength to do it. God will be your strength.

THE PASSAGE

We see a lot of success stories in the Bible, don't we? Ones like Moses crossing the Red Sea on dry land and David killing Goliath with three small stones. We see the walls of Jericho falling and fire and manna raining down from heaven.

These are exciting to study because we see the victory. We didn't have to wait for years or flee from the Egyptians like the Israelites. We just get to read about it and then a few verses later, hooray, it is finished and done.

I like to think of the victory we see as the other side of the wall. Take the exodus for example. The Israelites' wall was the Red Sea. God moved it, they walked to the other side, and then they wandered in the wilderness for the next forty years.

The benefit we have when looking at Scripture is that we see what is on the other side of the wall . . . for them. But for most of us right now, we can't see what's on the other side of our wall. And perhaps you're imagining the worst, like I was. You're what-ifing your wall to death, imagining all the worst possible scenarios that could come from jumping over—or even attempting to.

What if you fail.

What if you're rejected.

What if you look silly.

What if other people don't like it.

What if other people don't like you.

But what would happen today if you dared to believe that God will make you strong enough to handle whatever is coming up? What would happen if you made the pivot right now from your own weaknesses to God's strength?

What I want you to hear today is that even our most powerful Bible heroes felt moments of great weakness. And although they were never alone with God, he also surrounded them with people that not only endured it with them but encouraged them too.

In Exodus 17 we find ourselves deep in the heart of the wilderness, meeting up with some of my favorites—Moses, Aaron, and Joshua. Moses is dealing with some unhappy and grumbling Israelites, and we all know how fun that probably was for him.

It was so fun that at one point he actually turned to the Lord and said, "'What shall I do with this people? They are almost ready to stone me.'" (Exodus 17:4)

> **WE ALL NEED TO PEOPLE TO SAY, YOU CAN DO THIS.**

By now they had been in the wilderness for years and everyone was getting tired—of the situation and of each other. I imagine it was like quarantine was in 2020—isolated and lonely, even if you were with your people. But the worst part was that there was no end in sight.

Meanwhile, on top of trying to lead these cranky people, Moses was also battling for their protection. In the desert, of all places.

Amalek, the grandson of Esau, came to fight against the people of Israel, likely for their territory.

> Moses said to Joshua, "Choose for us men, and go out and fight with Amalek. Tomorrow I will stand on the top of the hill with the staff of God in my hand." So Joshua did as Moses told him, and fought with

Amalek, while Moses, Aaron, and Hur went up to the top of the hill. Whenever Moses held up his hand, Israel prevailed, and whenever he lowered his hand, Amalek prevailed. But Moses' hands grew weary, so they took a stone and put it under him, and he sat on it, while Aaron and Hur held up his hands, one on one side, and the other on the other side. So his hands were steady until the going down of the sun. And Joshua overwhelmed Amalek and his people with the sword. (Exodus 17:9-13)

Moses was weary. Moses, the guy who delivered the Israelites from the Egyptians and worked all the plagues and delivered the Ten Commandments and saw the glory of God walk by. That guy—he got weary too.

Maybe you're at a place in your life where you feel weary. You've been fighting for quite a while, you've been wandering in the desert for a while, you've been hiding your secret for a while. And now you're staring up at a giant wall thinking, there is no way you'll ever make it over this in one piece. And not only that, but you're afraid of what could possibly be on the other side.

I see you, friend, and I've been there a million times too. But I want you to look back at that passage of Scripture and notice what God did for Moses in his moment of weariness.

First, God gave people to hold his arms up.

God created us for community, and that community is often a God-given source of strength. Just like I needed Jeff to tell me, "You can do this" when that wall almost beat me, we all need people to say, "You can do this." Right from the beginning of creation, before sin entered the world, God saw that we need each other.

"Then the Lord God said, 'It is not good that the man should be alone; I will make him a helper fit for him.'" (Genesis 2:18) Then God created woman out of man, for man. For a partnership.

But with or without marriage, it was still not good for man to be alone. We see the need for community all over Scripture, necessary and good friendships (along with ones that are not good).

And in this story of battle with Moses, God places his two trusted friends next to him in battle. Notice they weren't fighting for him, or instead of him. They were helping him win the battle for others.

This is what is so beautiful about community. Everyone's fight looks different. Some of us are fighting for our marriages; some are fighting for our health or our mental health. Some of us are fighting for our kids, fighting for our faith, fighting for our financial well-being.

But we could all use someone to hold our arms up every once in a while.

In Matthew Henry's Concise Commentary of the Bible, he writes, "The strongest arm will fail with being long held out; it is God only whose hand is stretched out still. We do not find that Joshua's hands were heavy in *fighting*, but Moses' hands were heavy in *praying*; the more spiritual any service is, the more apt we are to fail and flag in it."[1] (emphasis mine)

I don't know about you, but I tend to beat myself up when I get tired. And girl, let me tell you that is a LOT of the time.

Even right now I am dead tired.

That's not even it.

I'm tired of being tired. Tired of feeling weak, tired of crying, tired of grieving. Tired of fighting and losing, battling shame, reasoning through actions. Tired of being angry, tired of forgiving, tired of trusting God.

But the Lord has richly given me women to hold my arms up in the battle. They do this by praying for me, encouraging me, reading these very words before they saw the light of day.

HAS GOD GIVEN YOU COMMUNITY, JUST NOT THE COMMUNITY YOU EXPECTED?

These kinds of friendships are never promised in Scripture. But often we miss out on people willing to do battle with us because we have our eyes fixated on the people we *want* to do battle with.

We think they need to look a certain way or have a certain career. We think they need to be like us or worse, be able to *do* something for us.

But God, in his great mercy and compassion, often puts

people in our path for reasons we may never know. And what if it's those very people that he will use to hold your arms up in battle?

So sweet weary one, if you are lonely in your battle and feel like God has not given you community, open your eyes. Look around you. Has he given you community, just not the community you expected?

A local church is a great place to find community. My deepest and most holy friendships were developed in the church right after I got married. I even have some dear friends from our youth group in high school that still encourage and pour into me—doing battle alongside of me.

And I know this might be an unpopular opinion, because we like to think that if God is going to make it happen, he will do it without our help, but a lot of times you have to take the first step to be available for friendship.

YOU HAVE TO MAKE YOURSELF AVAILABLE FOR FRIENDSHIP.

I often tell the story of being a new kindergarten mom in the carpool line at our school. I was lonely and isolated, desperate for meaningful friendships but without a means to get them—or so I thought. Every day I would drive through that carpool line to pick up our oldest son from kindergarten. And every day I would see this same group of cute moms laughing and smiling together by the back door of school.

I would think, "Oh, how nice of them to have friends. But what's so wrong with me that they're so stuck on leaving me out."

You see what's wrong with that statement, don't you? I mean, how would they even know that I existed when I kept lingering around the parking lot in my car?

I remember on a cold afternoon while I was enjoying the car's seat heater during pickup, the Lord stirred in my heart, "Get out of the car, Becky." I wish I could say that I'm the kind of girl who obeys immediately, but that would be all too generous of me.

Instead I argued. I waited a few days—weeks, even. But eventually I got out of the car, one hundred percent positive that I would be rejected.

"Hi. I don't know if you remember me, but I'm Brady's mom. He's in Mrs. Walzel's class . . ."

"Oh goodness, Amelia loves Brady!"

"Eli talks about Brady all the time!"

"I think Hannah has a crush on him!"

Immediately, I was met with graciousness. These women were apparently in search of the same thing I was—authentic friendship. But I would never have known that or seen the opportunity for it if I had stayed in my car.

And the women I met that day are the same women God used to gird me up for this battle. To give me strength when I felt like I couldn't keep going, to encourage me, and build me up.

Look around you.

Has God given you community to hold your arms up when you're tired of fighting? It may not look like a huge group of people you "do life wiih" or have birthday parties or playdates but notice that all Moses needed was three people. One on each side to hold his arms and one to keep fighting in front of him. I would bet that God has given that to you, and if you cannot see it, think outside of the box.

Find a mentor, a counselor, a friend, a spouse. A mom, a mom-figure, a Bible study leader and be bold in asking for help. Moses must have acknowledged his arms growing weak at some point, and he must have let his friends help.

———————

Back to Moses.

So God gave him community to get through the battle. But he also gave him a place to sit.

Have you ever worked all day and sat down to dinner and realized you never sat down once?

We've all likely had those kinds of chaotic days. But do you ever feel that way in your spiritual life too? Have you ever wondered when it was going to be over . . . when the battle would be done and finished so you could just move on?

Friend, it's okay to sit down, to grab a bottle of water, to rest. But it's not okay to quit.

We see throughout the Scriptures many times of withdraw, rest, refreshment. Jesus withdrew after working miracles and giving sermons. Paul withdrew years after coming to know Jesus as his savior to prepare for his ministry.

While rest seems to be the antithesis of strength, God often uses it as the source of our strength.

Fighting while resting continuously points to Christ as the source of our victory because it is so opposite of how the world tells us to fight.

More hustle, more work, more doors knocked on, more followers, more posts, more emails. That's what the world tells us. That's the recipe for success that culture gives us.

But what we see in this passage is that strength, and ultimately our victory, does not come from the hustle but from the holiness of rest.

DON'T BELIEVE THE LIE THAT YOU HAVE TO DO IT ALL.

Y'all, even God rested.

Not only did he rest, but he dedicated an *entire* day to rest. It's a natural rhythm that can, if we let it, give us strength when dedicated to God.

It is okay to be weary, friend. Of fighting, of praying, of standing and holding your arms up.

But don't quit. Don't believe the lie you're alone or have to do it all. God has given you community and rest. He will be your strength when you feel weak.

THE PIVOT

I don't think any of us enjoy feeling weak. We avoid it and don't admit it. But according to Paul in the New Testament, weakness is a good thing.

Let's fast forward to Paul's second letter to the Corinthians.

The apostle is helping build the church while also dealing with a "thorn" in his side. We never know what kind of thorn—perhaps it was a disease, maybe it was a temptation to sin or even a consequence of sin —but we know it was a burden God never removed.

Yet Paul's attitude towards it is striking. He writes to the church in Corinth,

> So to keep me from becoming conceited because of the surpassing greatness of the revelations, a thorn was given me in the flesh, a messenger of Satan to harass me, to keep me from becoming conceited. Three times I pleaded with the Lord about this, that it should leave me. But he said to me, "My grace is sufficient for you, for my power is made perfect in weakness." Therefore I will boast all the more gladly of my weaknesses, so that the power of Christ may rest upon me. For the sake of Christ, then, I am content with weaknesses, insults, hardships, persecutions, and calamities. For when I am weak, then I am strong.
>
> (2 Corinthians 12:7-10)

Paul immediately (or perhaps *eventually*) recognized that this weakness kept him humble.

Paul was a minister of the gospel. He wrote a majority of the New Testament, built the church, and invested in other ministers of the gospel. And yet he was weak, just like Moses.

We need to realize that weakness is not the enemy. Unbelief is.

Remember the wall I talked about at the beginning of this chapter? Could God have supernaturally lifted me up and over the wall? Well, I guess he could have. But he didn't. Not because he wasn't able, but because he wanted me to keep going. Part of our job here on earth is to keep putting one foot in front of the other—even in our weakness.

WEAKNESS IS NOT THE ENEMY. UNBELIEF IS.

Our weaknesses reminds us of our eternal need for God; they force our dependence on him. Even the most independent person cannot do everything on their own. And the choice we have to make when we feel weak, when we doubt we can move another muscle forward in our battle, is whether we will believe God will provide the strength to carry us through.

Whether through community, rest, or just flat-out physical strength to do what we think is impossible, we can believe that *God* is our strength because he already has been so many times before.

God shines the brightest in our weakness, our weariness, our exhaustion.

It is when we know that we couldn't *possibly* have made it through that day or done that thing or finished that task without God intervening, that we understand *his* strength in us all the more. This is what it means to be strong when we are weak.

And this is the pivot. To choose to reach out for help, to sit down, to not give up even when all feels lost.

Don't stop praying; don't stop leaning on the Lord. Pivot from your exhaustion back to the Lord's strength every time you'd rather quit. Remember that *nothing* is impossible with God. Even if it's hard.

10 | BELIEVING GOD'S WAY IS BETTER
even when it flat-out sucks

Two weeks after the intervention I met my dad for coffee. We sat over eggs and coffee at a local diner as he repeatedly said, "I'm sorry."

That breakfast was the closure I didn't know I needed. It was the first time I had seen him since the night I tore everything down—the night my heart burst wide open, laid bare for all to see. The same night that left me bruised, torn, and broken by someone I loved so deeply. The same man who had given me a life, a home, food, a college education.

When I walked into the restaurant that morning, he looked terrible. In the short two weeks since I had seen him, he'd obviously lost weight and the color on his face was now ashen. I hugged him tightly, even while he stood stiff and awkward. I ordered fresh coffee. My hand shook while

"I COULD SEE IT CLEARLY NOW— THE ABUSE, MY FATHER, AND MYSELF.

pouring cream into the steaming black cup. I couldn't *possibly* be this nervous around my dad.

But I was.

He was no longer the person I built up in my head for all those years. The elephant that had always stood between us was no longer obstructing my view. I could see it clearly now—the abuse, my father, and myself. I identified more about him in this brief moment at breakfast than I had my entire life.

He sat before me saying, "I'm sorry" but not apologizing. He said, "I love you" but wasn't loving. He said, "Thank you for forgiving me" but didn't need my forgiveness.

And finally, by the grace of a good God, the dam that had always held the longing for his approval broke.

Shortly after, he stopped contacting me. Since our family no longer provided the picture he wanted the world to see, we became irrelevant. Even if it took me years to understand that.

My sister and I received a few cards in the mail for a month or two following "The Intervention." They seemed vague and insincere, if I'm being honest. In fact, I have one in my hand at the moment, and it says, "It's my fault. I am repentant." We would also get text messages that said, "I remain willing to have a relationship with you."

There were a few things wrong with what was happening, the first one being that *I* should have been the one saying I was willing (or not willing) to have a relationship. After much therapy I became aware that this is typical of these kinds of offenders. Even in the most subtle of ways, they try to put their offense—*their* wrong, *their* mess—back onto the offended's shoulders.

The second troublesome thing with his communication was that although he *said* he was repentant, it didn't mean he actually was. In my experience, and from what I've seen in Scripture, repentance is shown not only by words, but by a change in posture and action. Repentance is taking steps to right the wrong, whatever that might look like. Repentance is falling prostrate before the Lord and your children, begging for forgiveness over specific things. Repentance is not a matter of saying sorry and then moving on like nothing ever happened. Being sorry and being sorry you got caught are two different things *entirely*.

Let me be clear, none of that "repentance" happened.

My heart was broken at his lack of remorse for what he had done. For the damage he had inflicted not only on me, but on our entire family. And I think what caused me the most pain at that time was that I was so willing, ready, and hopeful that we would be able to have an entire new relationship together—the relationship I had always wanted.

But after a few months of "I'm repentant" texts, I stopped responding. I had nothing more to say other than "I got your card" or "I got your text." What was I supposed to do with a card that says, "It is my fault," but that also made it clear he did not want to address the issue itself and get help? I couldn't move forward like that.

It was the beginning of July 2018 when I sent my last text.

I WAS GOING TO CHOOSE TO BELIEVE THAT GOD'S WAY WAS BETTER FOR ME IN THE LONG RUN.

I was sitting on the very couch that I'm sitting on now and through tears, I sent a message telling him I wasn't ready for a relationship, but that also wanted to make sure he was physically okay. My worst nightmare was that he would harm himself or that something would happen to him, and none of us would know. I was beyond worried and just needed to know he was okay for my own well-being.

I waited for the dots to appear. It felt like hours that I sat and stared at my phone, clicking on the screen, making sure I didn't miss a message back. I sat, I cried, I prayed, and I waited.

And I didn't hear from him at all for over a year..

I was so disappointed.

I was disappointed that all the "what ifs" about who he really was actually turned out to be true. I was devastated that he didn't want me, but that he wanted the facade of a family. He wanted to *appear* a certain way to the world—a Sunday school teacher, a choir member, a deacon, a father, a husband, a hard worker. But, it was all fake, all for show, all for him.

As much as I wanted to bust through the boundaries I had mentally set and go around what the Lord had called me to do, I was determined to not manipulate the situation. I was going to choose to believe that God's way was better for me in the long run, even if I didn't like it right now.

I didn't understand God's ways then, and I don't understand them any more today.

I don't understand why God takes godly men before their time but leaves ones who wreak havoc.

I don't understand why God allows some women to get pregnant and not others.

I don't understand why God gives some kids good families and not others.

I don't understand why God allows the things he allows. I don't think I ever will.

But this is when it is *pivotal* that I choose to believe he is who he says he is.

Sometimes life doesn't make sense. It's difficult and I question everything that's going on around me. And I certainly don't feel like everything is "fair."

But what I do know is that God is good, he is for me (and for you), and his way is better than my way (even if it doesn't feel like it in the moment.)

THE PASSAGE

The story of Abram and Sarai sticks out to me when I think God's way is confusing and impossible. Their story can be found throughout several pages of the Bible, but let's focus on Genesis chapter 15.

Abram was a descendant of Noah—a descendant way down the genealogical line.

We are first introduced to him when Abram's father Terah took him, his wife Sarai, and his nephew Lot from Ur into the land of Canaan where they settled. Immediately God tells Abram, "'I will make you a great nation, and I will bless you and make your name great, so that you will be a blessing. . . And Abram believed the Lord, and he counted it to him as righteousness." (Genesis 12:2, 15:6)

Abram's belief was counted to him as *righteousness*. Not his perfection, not his willingness to go, not even his obedience that came from his belief. It was his belief.

If it were me in this situation, my first response would not be belief but millions of questions. "But how is this going to happen for me, Lord? What are you going to do and what should I do? What do I need to do tomorrow, but also what will this look like for me in a few years?"

Listen, I want to be the girl who obeys immediately. I want to be the girl who says, "as you will, Lord," but I am just not. I have all the questions and all the concerns, and I most definitely let the Lord know my position from the get-go. But what I love so much in this passage of Scripture is that Abram was immediately obedient. Abram immediately believed God's promise. So much so that he *acted* on it.

Soon Abram and Lot separate and while Lot has his own set of problems, God comes to Abram again and tells him, "'Look toward heaven, and number the stars, if you are able to number them.' Then he said to him, 'So shall your offspring be.'" (Genesis 15:5) Gosh, I love how God talks sometimes.

The thing you should know about Abram at this point is that he was already old, and maybe more significantly, so was Sarai. In fact, Abram had previously reminded God about their age right before God told Abram his descendants would outnumber the stars just in case God had forgotten. (This sounds *way* more like me.)

> # I DOUBT WHAT I HEARD, I DOUBT MY DIRECTION, I DOUBT GOD.

But God had told Abram on multiple occasions that his age didn't matter. Somehow, he would have offspring that outnumbered the stars, and they would then become a great nation. No matter what Abram thought was or wasn't possible.

Oh, but then came lots of waiting. Lots and lots of waiting, and if I'm being honest, I don't like waiting for anything, let alone a promise God has given to me. There are many times that God tells me to wait, then I look down at my calendar before I think, okay, I'll wait. But then when enough time has passed, or perhaps it feels a bit like God has forgotten the thing, or the waiting time becomes more of a wait-some-more type of thing, I begin to doubt. I doubt what I heard, I doubt my direction, I doubt God.

I like to trick myself into thinking maybe it is my turn to do something . . . maybe I'm not *supposed* to wait anymore. Maybe it's time to act. After all, Jesus did ask Peter to get out of the boat so that he could walk on the water. I mean, maybe God is waiting on me?

But sometimes, y'all, the wait is just a wait. Sometimes it is simply wait some more. And then some more. And that is not comfortable for me, nor was it comfortable for Abram and Sarai.

"Now Sarai, Abram's wife, had borne him no children. She had a female Egyptian servant whose name was Hagar. And Sarai said to Abram, 'Behold now, the Lord has prevented me from bearing children. Go in to my servant; it may be that I shall obtain children by her.' And Abram listened to the voice of Sarai." (Genesis 16:1-2)

(Just to be clear, when Scripture tells us that Abram went *in* to Hagar, it means exactly what you think it means.)

Sarai thought she knew better than God. She believed the promises he had given to Abram but was either tired of waiting or thought God was waiting on her. But he wasn't waiting on her, rather asking her to wait on him.

When God gave Abram the promise about his offspring, he listened to the voice of Sarai instead.

He tried to manipulate his waiting time. He (and Sarai) believed they knew better than the Lord, and they acted on that belief. The nation God was talking about wasn't going to come through a man making his own way but through a very old man and woman trusting God to make a way.

What we learn from Abram here is that when God gives us a promise, he doesn't expect *us* to see it to fruition. Rather, he gives us a promise and *he* brings it to fruition. In his timing and in his way.

So the question is, do you believe the Lord or the voice of someone else?

THE PIVOT

My heart is *still* torn over the broken relationship with my father. It takes a lot of energy to be brokenhearted, and there were many times, especially at the beginning, when I felt like none of this was worth it and I wanted my father back. I wanted to return to my old life with uncomplicated holidays, and low expectations, and compartmentalized emotions.

But then I remember that God's way is better than mine, even when I can't see it and can't explain it. I remember the story of Sarai and I think to myself, *I don't want to mess this wait up.* Yes, I'm still waiting to see what God will do. I haven't seen the reconciliation or redemption I prayed for, but I have seen God make good of all the things I've messed up.

Just like God did for Abram and Sarai.

Despite Abram listening to the voice of his wife, God followed through on his word. Sarai gave birth to Isaac and through him, Abram became the father of the Israelites, the people so much of Scripture is written to and about.

> **MANIPULATING OUR WAITING TIME DOESN'T CREATE A BETTER SOLUTION. IT CREATES DISAPPOINTMENT.**

As for Hagar, Abram had a baby with her, but it should come as no surprise that this is not how the nation of Israel was founded.

Instead, Scripture tells us that Sarai looked on Hagar with resentment and bitterness. Sarai treated Hagar so terribly that Hagar fled into the wilderness convinced that she and her child would eventually die. Manipulating our waiting time doesn't create a better solution. It creates disappointment.

Waiting on God is not fun. It's not fun when you know what you're waiting on, and maybe even more so when you don't. Yet we all come to this point when we must pivot from the wait to a belief that God's way is, despite what we might understand, better than our own.

In Isaiah, God says to Abram's descendants,

Seek the Lord while he may be found; call upon him

while he is near; let the wicked forsake his way and the unrighteous man his thoughts; let him return to the Lord, that he may have compassion on him, and to our God, for he will abundantly pardon. For my thoughts are not your thoughts, neither are your ways my ways, declares the Lord. For as the heavens are higher than the earth, so are my ways higher than your ways and my thoughts than your thoughts. (Isaiah 55:6-9)

Of course I would rather my father sincerely apologize and my family be reconciled with a Hallmark movie ending. I could absolutely focus on what *isn't* happening. I could manipulate the situation and tell my father exactly what he needs to do, step by step, and get a false (and unhealthy) relationship with him. I could violate my new healthy boundaries and continue not addressing the issue at hand.

But instead, I choose to believe God's way is better. Even if it's a choice I have to make repeatedly throughout my day.

The difficulty is that I really might never understand why.

I might *never* know what's happening on the other side of those boundaries, what my father is or isn't working out a few towns over. I might die never having talked with him again, and that, my friend, is an incredibly difficult reality to swallow.

But also, it all might change tomorrow. God might do

something new, and I'll be finished waiting. He might work it out in a way that I'll be able to see the reason for the wait.

Either way, I will continue choosing to believe that God's ways are better than mine . . . even when they flat out suck.

11 | BELIEVING GOD CAN

even when he doesn't

I wanted nothing more than for my parents to stay together. In my therapy sessions at the very beginning, my counselor had asked me, "What do you think would happen if you told your mom about this?" She was trying to get me to address all the elephants in the room. The very same reasons why I had convinced myself to never acknowledge the truth of my abuse.

After taking a deep, carefully calculated breath, I responded, "The worst thing that could happen would be that parents get divorced." I sat on the couch in a puddle of tears as I mumbled my way through that sentence.

I couldn't imagine this scenario in my life.

It would be soul crushing. But I knew God could prevent this from happening; I knew that he was far beyond able to provide healing in their marriage.

I cried, I pleaded, I got down on my face before God. I begged God to heal. I begged God to intervene. I begged God to work miracles in their relationship and in our family, giving us reconciliation and restoration.

> **KNOWING THAT GOD COULD RESTORE OUR FAMILY WITH JUST A WORD AND YET DOESN'T IS ONE OF THE HARDEST PILLS I'VE EVER HAD TO SWALLOW.**

But he didn't.

At thirty-six years old, my dad moved out. And as much as I trusted that this was the right decision for all involved, I had to be honest and admit that this was the very thing I had prayed against for months. This was the opposite of what I wanted, and certainly wasn't what I had in mind when I was begging God for restoration, peace, and healing. This was the thing I had spent countless hours begging God *not* to do.

And yet this is where we were.

I was devastated, heartbroken, and sad, but most of all, I was angry.

I was angry I'd listened to all the people who said, "God would work it out." I was angry at the Scriptures I read that said, "God works everything for good" and that he would give me the desires of my heart. I was angry that God would allow something he said he hated, that he wouldn't make us all just feel better when we knew that he could.

But most of all, I was angry at God himself.

Knowing that God *could* restore our family with just a word and yet doesn't is one of the hardest pills I've ever swallowed. Knowing he could, in a split second, heal someone in your life, but disease still remains rampant, makes it increasingly difficult to believe the God of the Bible is the compassionate, almighty miracle worker that he so often claims to be.

Maybe you're here today.

You've been begging God to intervene in some way. You've cried out, you've fasted, you've prayed. You're waiting for direction to move. You're waiting on healing to take place. You're waiting on a relationship to be restored. You're waiting on a spouse to come back. You're waiting on a job to say yes. You're waiting on that door to open, that treatment to do its thing, or for that child to make a better choice.

And you know, beyond a shadow of a doubt, that God is *able*. You know that he could change the outcome, he could force someone's hands, he could part the Red Sea and rain manna down from Heaven for you if he wanted to. But he doesn't.

And so you're struggling.

Girl, that's okay.

I understand what it's like to not be okay with what

God is doing. What he's allowing. I understand what it's like to be in the middle of a forever wait, wondering if God will ever come through, living in the tension of what you want and what he's not doing. I understand how difficult it can be to make sense of what Scripture tells you about God being good and loving and kind, when all it feels like right now is that he is cold, distant, and doesn't care one bit.

I get it.

But.

Let me whisper a sweet word of encouragement—you are not the only one. *We* are not the only ones who struggle with this. We are not the only ones who have felt like God has left us, doing for everyone else but not us.

And despite what it might feel like, God has a plan more magnificent than we could ever think or imagine. And if we will just believe him, we might see it.

To be honest, this is probably one of the more difficult chapters of this book to write. There's not a conclusion here for me. There's no happy ending, no "let me tell you what to do because it all worked out for me" conclusion to this chapter . . . or even this book.

And so, I write this from a place of waiting. Waiting on God to do the thing—or just *something*—to heal, restore, or provide peace. Waiting to see God's plan come to light, waiting to see the little miracles along the way.

So don't for one second think that I've got it all figured out. Don't stop reading because *you're* still waiting, and you think *I've* moved on. I haven't. We haven't. God hasn't. He still has me here, and I'm assuming you're still here too.

And in the waiting, it's hard for me *not* to get stuck in a place where I tell God, "If only you would do what I want this would all be better."

Some of Jesus's favorite people were in that place too.

THE PASSAGE

You may have heard about the story of Mary and Martha. This monumental story in the Bible, housed in just five short verses, is often used at women's retreats. Entire Bible studies, books, and curriculum have been devoted to this one story, talking about the difference between Mary and Martha.

If you are unfamiliar, you can find the short story in Luke 10:38-41. The summary of it is that Jesus was making his way through a village after performing miracles and teaching. Martha welcomed Jesus into her house along with her sister Mary. Martha was the hostess with the mostess, doing everything she could to make her home an inviting and welcoming place for the Lord Jesus. And, I mean, I don't blame her.

I imagine her cooking and cleaning, putting toilet paper in the bathroom, and picking up the rogue Lego or two. Obviously, this is a modern-day version, but we've all been there, am I right? A last-minute visit from someone, let alone *Jesus*, would send most of us into a tizzy.

But the story tells us that Martha was "distracted with

much serving" while Mary was sitting at the feet of Jesus, listening to his teaching. (Luke 10:40) There is so much to unpack here, but basically, Jesus winds up telling the ladies that Mary chose the better part—to sit with him.

A LOT OF WHAT GOD DOES DOESN'T MAKE SENSE TO ME.

We don't know if this was the first time they had met, or if they had grown up together. We don't know how Mary and Martha's brother Lazarus played a role in this story of service and sitting. But we do know that, at some point, Jesus and Lazarus became very close friends.

Later on, while Jesus was ministering elsewhere, Lazarus became ill. "So the sisters sent to him saying, 'Lord, he whom you love is ill.'" (John 11:3) I imagine they knew full well what Jesus was capable of. They knew he could hurry back to heal their brother whom he loved.

They trusted Jesus. They believed in Jesus *and* believed Jesus. They expected him to do for them what they had seen him do for others.

> "But when Jesus heard it, he said, 'This illness does not lead to death. It is for the glory of God, so that the Son of God may be glorified through it.'" (John 11:4)

I don't know about you, but if I had heard those words, I would have thought, "Awesome. God's got this. Lazarus is going to be just fine." I would have heard those words and immediately felt better. I would have expected Jesus to come running to heal my brother. After all, he just said, "This illness does *not* lead to death."

But the very next verse always surprises me. John writes, "Now Jesus loved Martha and her sister and Lazarus. So, when he heard that Lazarus was ill, he stayed two days longer in the place where he was." (John 11:5-6)

What did he just say?

He loved this family, so he stayed two days *longer*? He loved this family, and he didn't drop everything that he was doing and immediately go heal him? This doesn't make sense to me.

The thing is that a lot of what God does doesn't make sense to me. Sure, there are many moments in my life where God does the unexpected, but there are also many more where he doesn't. He doesn't heal, he doesn't return, he doesn't restore.

He doesn't drop everything he's doing to fix the situation in front of me, just like with Lazarus.

After those two days of staying to minister, Jesus told his disciples to pick up and go back to Judea. The men argue with him because the Jews were seeking to stone him for the message he was preaching. After much debate, Jesus finally lets them in.

He tells them, "'Lazarus has died, and for your sake I am glad that I was not there, so that you may believe. But let us go to him." (John 11:14-15)

Okay. So Jesus knows Lazarus has died, and then says it was *good* that he was not there? Let's visit that one more time—Jesus waited until Lazarus *died* to go to him.

It doesn't make sense to the one who doesn't know Jesus. Even if you haven't heard this story before, but if you know a little about Jesus, you might see where this story is headed.

He waited so that the disciples would believe. He waited so that God would be glorified, just like he said at the very beginning.

"Now when Jesus came, he found that Lazarus had already been in the tomb four days. . .. So when Martha heard that Jesus was coming, she went and met him, but Mary remained seated in the house." (Mary does a lot of sitting it seems.) "Martha said to Jesus, 'Lord, if you had been here, my brother would not have died.'" (John 11:17, 20-21)

If you had been here.

Can you imagine her disappointment that her brother had died? Not only had he died, but it seemed that Jesus had not come through the way he said he would.

Disappointed.

Grieving.

Let down.

Have you been there? Have you begged God for something only for him to deny it?

What if, though, it's not that he isn't coming through or holding up his end of the deal? What if he has something better planned? What if your loss is a loss that doesn't lead to death but leads to the glorification of the kingdom of God? What if your grief is part of God's bigger plan for someone else to believe?

Martha then says to Jesus, "'But even now I know that whatever you ask from God, God will give you.'" (John 11:22)

She *still* believed.

Even after her brother died. Even after it seemed that Jesus didn't do what he said he would. Even after he waited three days and she thought if only he had been there, it wouldn't have happened at all.

She believed.

Jesus then tells her that her brother will rise again. I imagine her rolling her eyes in her grief before saying, "'I know that he will rise again in the resurrection on the last day.'" (John 11:24) She assumed she knew what he was talking about.

Martha called her sister out, telling her that Jesus had arrived. She goes to Jesus, falls at his feet, and repeats the same sentiment that Martha had, "'Lord, if you had been here, my brother would not have died.'" (John 11:32)

The sisters wept, and Jesus wept right alongside of them. Scripture tells us that "he was deeply moved in his spirit and greatly troubled." (John 11:33) He felt compassion for them. He understood it. He was fully human while also fully God. He knew what they were going through and grieved not only for them, but alongside of them.

Scripture tells us that God is near to the brokenhearted.

He keeps our tears in a bottle, counting every one. There is a season for everything, and one of those is mourning.

When our spirit grieves, when our hearts are ripped to pieces, God grieves with us. He does not want to see us brokenhearted and lonely. He doesn't want us to experience the loss and the brokenness of the world. But at the same time, he sees the bigger picture and understands the greater good.

God tells us in Isaiah, "For my thoughts are not your thoughts, neither are your ways my ways, declares the Lord. For as the heavens are higher than the earth, so are my ways higher than your ways and my thoughts than your thoughts." (Isaiah 55:8-9)

WHILE OUR SCOPE AND VISION ARE LIMITED, HIS IS ALL ENCOMPASSING.

His plan for our lives reaches far before and beyond our own. He allows things *now* that have impact beyond our lifetime. We suffer consequences and benefits from things, circumstances, and people who came before us.

And while our scope of vision is limited, God's is all-encompassing. He knows what is for our good, yes, but he also knows what is for *his* good. For the good of the kingdom. For his glory.

Eventually, Jesus came to the tomb of Lazarus and

called him to come out. "The man who had died came out, his hands and feet bound with linen strips, and his face wrapped with a cloth." (John 11:44)

I imagine that when people heard Lazarus was raised from the dead, they not only believed *in* Jesus, but believed Jesus.

I imagine that when the story reached the far ends of the earth in their day, that people had to see the miraculous healing power of Jesus.

And I imagine that more people came to believe in the Lord Jesus Christ through Lazarus's death and resurrection than would have through his miraculous healing.

THE PIVOT

Martha didn't doubt Jesus's *ability* to heal, but she did doubt his methods. She said, "If only you had been here."

I've said that much of my life.

If only God had been there to protect me from my father.

If only God had been there to provide reconciliation.

Maybe you've said a version of that too.

If only God had been there, I would not have gone up to that hotel room.

If only God had been there, I wouldn't have said yes to that drink.

If only God had been there, my son wouldn't have died.

If only God had been there, I would have gotten this

job.

If only.

I don't know a lot of things, but I do know this to be true: God loves you and has plans and purposes for your life. I know that his plans are *good*, not to harm you but to give you hope in a future.

I also know that he is at work in his kingdom. I know that we live in a broken world, one in which we experience the effects of brokenness and sin. We suffer consequences that are not our own, and we make bad choices that affect generations.

But God can and will use it all. *Eventually.*

Perhaps it won't be how we ask or the way that we want him to. Maybe we won't ever see how it works out for good—but we were never promised that vision. We were just promised that it will.

And we have to choose, like it or not, to believe him for that.

Even when we don't see, and especially when we don't feel it.

Believing that God is *capable* and believing that he will are two different things. Believing that he will—or at least, *eventually* will—is not a false hope. It is the reality that roots us in our faith. That one day we will meet Jesus face to face and all the brokenness of the world will be over. The pain and pressure of the world will grow dim in the light of his glory, and we will one day understand that the small parts we played, while important to the Lord, were minuscule in comparison to the glory of the kingdom.

I still hold out hope for reconciliation, although I hope for it in a different way. I hope that my father experiences the grace of Jesus at some point in his life—that he will truly understand the power and the peace of the gospel. I hope for my mom to experience the adoration of a man, although I know, and she knows, that her value comes from Jesus and Jesus alone.

And I hope that every day I can see something good that has come out of God allowing something tragic in my life.

> **BECAUSE OF THIS HOPE, I CAN PIVOT FROM DISAPPOINTMENT TO FAITH.**

Because of this hope, I can pivot from disappointment to the knowledge of faith, choosing to believe that not only is God capable but he is true to his promises. For me, for you, and for them.

WHAT THEN SHALL WE SAY TO THESE THINGS? IF GOD IS FOR US, WHO CAN BE AGAINST US?

romans 8:31

12 | BELIEVING GOD IS FOR YOU
not just for everyone else

We all know those people. The ones who are successful at everything. The ones who touch something, anything, and it turns to gold. The ones who start an Instagram account and the next day have 1.2 million followers. The ones who post a random video that goes viral. The ones who get a job as a factory worker but end up running the factory two months later.

My husband is one of those people.

He's totally going to kill me for including this, but the truth will preach, am I right? My husband, Jeff, is the kind of guy who walks into a room full of people and everyone stops to talk to him. He's the guy who goes after what he wants and gets it, the kind who has won every election he's ever ran for (starting with 5th grade class president) and gotten every part he auditioned for.

I'm not saying that he hasn't worked for it, because my gosh, he absolutely has. And I'm not saying that he doesn't deserve every position or every award that he's received, because goodness knows I am his biggest fan.

> **JESUS NEVER TAUGHT HIS DISCIPLES TO HUSTLE. HE TAUGHT THEM TO REST.**

I love this magnetic sort of thing about him. I really do.

But me? I'm not one of those people.

I'm the person who has submitted too many book proposals to count. I'm the girl who hasn't gotten the job, who doesn't network well, who gets forgotten and left out often. I'm the person who meets someone three or four times before they recognize my name.

I'm the girl who works her tail off and doesn't get the thing, doesn't see the results, doesn't see growth.

And truth be told, I'm tired of the whole "hustle gospel." The women who preach that if we just want it bad enough, work hard enough, hustle long enough, God will give us all our dreams and more.

The truth is, God doesn't work that way. Jesus never taught his disciples to hustle. He taught them to *rest*. More specifically, to rest in him.

Years ago, I was invited to a networking event for

women in ministry. I was so excited because I was starting a new ministry called FreeToo with a few of my friends and I wanted to learn from other women who had gone before me. I knew I couldn't do it alone, nor did I want to.

I was looking forward to insight, inspiration, advice, prayer. But more than that, I was looking forward to making friends with other women in ministry. I was hoping to have people to link arms with, to offer wisdom and words of encouragement.

My expectations were high.

I showed up that morning nervous but excited. I had prayed my entire drive into the city that God would go before me and give me words to say and a humble heart to learn and glean from these more seasoned women.

I walked in not knowing a soul since the woman who had invited me had not arrived yet. I was graciously greeted by the host and shown the coffee and snacks. I smiled and said thank you as she went to greet another guest.

Immediately I felt like a fish out of water, women chatting around me but never to me. I took a deep breath and preached to myself what I often preach to my daughter, "You have to include yourself to be included."

So I walked up to a group of women and introduced myself.

Anxiety quickly took over as I stumbled over my words and any sort of description of what I do. *Am I an artist? Am I a teacher? Am I a writer?* At that point I didn't even know what to say other than "I'm so glad to meet you."

I quickly excused myself to grab a cup of coffee—you know, just what I needed to calm my escalating nerves.

As I was figuring out the fancy Keurig situation on the counter, I recognized a younger girl who was standing close but had just walked in. I introduced myself and we started talking. As it turned out, we had a lot of mutual friends, and she had recently taken an exciting new role in ministry.

We talked for a long while, and thinking back on it now, perhaps I monopolized her time, but I was just so happy to have made a connection. I gave her my business card, we swapped information, and the program got started.

As I left that day, I felt incredibly grateful to have made a connection with this one woman. Sure, I met several other women who said how lovely it was to meet me, but when it came time to swap numbers, they hesitated. I get it, I really do. Time is valuable, and no one can meet, mentor, disciple, or pray with every person they meet.

I one hundred percent know this to be true. I understand this. Truly.

But that one connection felt, well, it felt *special*. God ordained. Sovereign. It felt like maybe, just perhaps, God was for me too.

The next day, I shot her a message saying it was nice to meet her and that I would be praying over her new position in ministry.

No response. No thumbs up. No "nice to meet you too."

A week or two later I sent another message, "I'd love to grab coffee when you have some time. . .."

No response. No thumbs up. Nothing.

Unfortunately, this isn't the first time this has happened to me. It's not the first time people have smiled and nodded and said the polite things in the moment but forgotten a conversation that I thought had been so meaningful.

And let's be honest, that stinks.

It makes me feel lonely, as though everyone else has found their group of people to minister with, to buddy up with, and I just can't.

Immediately, my thoughts go to "what's wrong with me" and "why don't they like me?"

SATAN WANTS TO KEEP US IN THESE MOMENTS OF ISOLATION.

They grow more constructive though as I turn back to the Lord and ask, "Am I not doing what you want me to do? Because listen, there's only so much I can do without you. You're going have to take it the rest of the way."

It's easy to look at everybody *else's* success and let my thoughts wander into "God is so obviously for them but he's just not for me" territory.

The thing is that nothing could be further from the truth.

Satan wants to keep us in these moments of isolation. He wants the lonely feeling to drive us away from God. Because if we are alone and far from God? Well, now, that's his recipe for the perfect storm.

The struggle to believe that God is *for* us doesn't necessarily come from thinking he's against us, but often from thinking he's for someone else more.

> **JUST BECAUSE YOU'RE STILL WAITING DOESN'T MEAN GOD IS FOR HER AND NOT FOR YOU.**

And girl, this is comparison in its most pure form. I used to believe I didn't struggle with comparison because I never said, "I want what she has." But the enemy was tricking me.

I was saying, "Why has God given her that thing and not given me this thing?" It's the same thought. Although I didn't want the same thing as someone else, I was comparing the God who gave her what she wanted to the God who didn't give me what I wanted.

You see what I'm saying?

Our God is one in the same. The God who gives success or opportunities to the girl next to you—even if they aren't the specific opportunities you want—is the same God you're still waiting on. And just because you're still waiting doesn't mean he is for *her* and not for *you*.

THE PASSAGE

One of my favorite people in Scripture is a man you've probably never heard of before. His name is Bezalel, and he is briefly introduced deep in the book of Exodus.

God was giving Moses incredibly specific instructions on how to build the temple, the ark of the covenant, and everything around it.

God told him how to consecrate the priests, offer sacrifices and what kind of incense they can use and when to use it. He told them what the priests can wear, what kind of oil they could use, what the altar would look like. I mean, I don't know if I could ever be that detail oriented.

But then they come to the actual building part. The blueprints. The plans.

I'm sure Moses was like, "This is great, God, but I have no idea how to build something like this. Remember? I lived in a palace most of my life." And the Lord says to Moses at what seemed like the perfect time:

"See, I have called by name Bezalel the son of Uri, son of Hur, of the tribe of Judah, and I have filled him with the Spirit of God, with ability and intelligence, with knowledge and all craftsmanship, to devise artistic designs, to work in gold, silver, and bronze, in cutting stones for setting, and in carving wood, to work in every craft." (Exodus 31:2-5)

What I find so beautiful here is that the Lord not only created Bezalel for this moment, but he had also filled him with ability, intelligence, and craftsmanship to complete it, along with the power of his spirit.

God prepared Bezalel to build all these things he had instructed.

When I first read this passage, I remember being

awestruck at God's attention to detail. I've always been fascinated with the backstory of people in the Bible. They just pop up out of nowhere, play whatever part they were meant to play, and then fade back into the background again.

But what's interesting here is that we know Bezalel had been *prepared* for this. We don't know if this was his dream—to build all these things for the Lord. We don't know if he was happy being a carpenter or if he longed to have a platform like Moses.

But we do know that Bezalel was created by God for this moment. And you were created with just as much detail too.

What do you suppose would have happened if Bezalel was like, "But I want to be doing what Moses is doing?" How would things have changed if Bezalel had gotten so caught up in wanting to serve God in the way that Moses or Joshua or Aaron were serving him instead of practicing the gifts and skills God had already instilled in him?

If he spent the years prior to this moment—prior to this call—longing to be something or somewhere else, my hunch is that he would not have been prepared for this moment. His skill may have been lacking, his attention to detail might have been frustrated or off. The way we get good at our skill is to *practice* our skill.

Whether it is on a stage or not.

Our problem here is not what we believe about God, it's how we measure his value of us.

I have not been able to find a place in the Bible where

God says the gift of leadership is more valuable than the gift of servitude. There isn't a place in Scripture that God tells us the one on the stage is more important than the one behind it. In fact, he leads us to believe the opposite when Jesus says that "the last will be first, and the first last." (Matthew 20:16)

BEZALEL WAS NEVER SUPPOSED TO BE MOSES. AND YOU'RE NOT SUPPOSED TO BE HER.

Bezalel wasn't going to receive the Ten Commandments like Moses or be the one leading people across dry land or bringing water from a huge rock. But, from what little we know, it seems like Bezalel had confidence that God had created him to be where and who and what he was. For that time, for that season, for that purpose.

Bezalel was never supposed to be Moses.

And you're not supposed to be her.

THE PIVOT

Maybe you're in a season of life when you feel like God is for everyone else and just not for you. You look around and see that everyone else is getting married, or has their dream job, or has the child that you're still waiting for. You compare your life to the girl across the street or on the other side of the screen. You think, *God is blessing her in this way, so he must be for her, but he's just not for me.*

But could it be that God is preparing you for a role he created *just for you*? Could it be that while you're waiting for this next opportunity, you are missing these other opportunities right under your nose? Could it be that God is asking you to be faithful with what you have—the skill set, the finances, the position, the community—before he gives you the other thing you think you're chasing? Could it be that he is giving you time to refine your gifts and practice skills before giving you a platform to use them on?

> **YOUR RACE DOESN'T LOOK LIKE HERS AND HER RACE DOESN'T LOOK LIKE MINE.**

Could it be that he created you so uniquely that there is no way you could compare what she is doing with what you will do? Could it be that the race God has marked out for you is so completely out of left field that you can't even comprehend what he is going to ask you to do?

Paul writes in his first letter to the Corinthians of the church, "For the body does not consist of one member but of many," meaning that we all play different roles in the kingdom of God. (1 Corinthians 12:14) He goes on to say, "If the foot should say, 'Because I am not a hand, I do not belong to the body,' that would not make it any less a part of the body." (1

Corinthians 12:15)

In other words, it doesn't matter if you are a hand or a foot or an eyeball—you have a role to play in the kingdom of God.

If God didn't have a part for you to play, if he didn't want to take you somewhere or use you in some capacity for the kingdom, you wouldn't even be here. We are told repeatedly in Scripture that God has plans for us, right? So that means he has plans for *you*. Your days and your race are marked out for you specifically. And your race doesn't look like hers and her race doesn't look like mine.

And that's okay. That does not mean that God is for her and not me. It doesn't mean that God is for you and not for her. It means that God has created each of us in his image with different talents, gifts, and abilities to be used for his glory.

And he is for each one of us.

Maybe you're a Bezalel in a Moses story.

Maybe it's time you stop believing that God is for her more than he is for you because she has a stage, followers, a husband, a network. You have to choose to believe that God has great plans and purposes for *your* life, and if you just keep your head down and walk in the calling that he has uniquely given you, then he will take you and do what he wants to do.

Whether the world thinks it's important or not.

———————

I am thankful to report that years later I have found some special women to do ministry with. Women who have mentored me, held me through tears, walked with me through all the highs and lows and still hang out on the other side with me. They're the women who remind me to believe that God is for me, even when it feels like I am unsuccessful, unnoticed, unimportant.

They're the women that I know God was preparing me for and preparing for me all along—even in those moments I felt rejected and alone.

My prayer for you today is that you would place more value on how God cares for you than how the world sees you. Maybe if we start to get that in order, we'll start believing it more too.

13 | BELIEVING GOD WILL REDEEM
even if he doesn't restore

Have you ever wanted something so badly you couldn't sleep? You know those gut-wrenching, heart-aching, life-stopping desires that come at you like a train about to go off the tracks?

That's how I felt about reconciliation with my father.

There was only one problem. Reconciliation would require two cooperative people, right? Like, I couldn't be the only one in the relationship who cared enough to pay attention. And for over thirty years, that had been exactly what our relationship was—my pursuit of him.

Of course, for most of my life, I didn't understand that wasn't a healthy parent-child relationship. In fact, it was the opposite of that. I didn't understand that I shouldn't be falling all over myself to keep the peace and make him happy, protecting him at every turn so no one else would get upset with him.

But when I finally was brave enough to acknowledge even the slight possibility of toxicity, my worst fear was realized—he left me.

Now, listen, my intention here is not to run my father or our relationship through the mud. My goal instead is to help the woman walking through something similar not feel alone.

MY WORST FEAR WAS REALIZED. HE LEFT ME.

Remember at the beginning when I said that I want you to know what it looks like in the middle of the mud and muck? I wanted to talk about choosing belief when everything isn't turning out like that Hallmark movie promised? And here we are.

I bet for a lot of you, if not for *most* of you even, there is at least one relationship in your life that you think is beyond reconciliation. A friendship, a marriage, a family relationship that you are praying and begging God to heal, but when you're being honest with yourself, you know it's most likely impossible.

For me, it's the relationship with my father.

So much of the trauma I now experience from those years of abuse is not from the physicality of the abuse itself. Instead, it's the fallout. The things I've taught myself as a result of being used for someone else's pleasure— as an object for someone else's enjoyment.

I know it might sound crazy to some, but the thing I wanted most after confronting the abuse was an honest relationship with my father. I wanted to be loved— genuinely loved— by the man who raised me and, I thought, was pretty much obligated to. *But he didn't.* And I was beginning to understand he probably never will.

I want to make it clear that our lack of relationship with him was not because we weren't willing. It was because we were willing with the addition of boundaries. We were willing to let him into our lives and build something new, not something that would be the same.

The saddest thing to me about it all was that so much life was happening without him. I started a ministry and shared my testimony of abuse publicly. I testified in a legislative hearing about extending the civil statute of limitations. My story was in the newspaper and on the radio and social media.

My brother and sister-in-law got pregnant. My oldest son started middle school and began playing the drums (well, I might add). My dad missed family vacations, birthdays, funerals and all the celebrations that go on with simply living our lives. He missed Father's Days and Mother's Days and Easters and Christmases.

And regardless of the nightmares I suffered, the sleepless and tear-filled nights that came with this new territory, I still held out hope that he would come back. Remorseful, repentant, contrite, and honest.

Have you hoped for something new in a relationship

too? Maybe there's infidelity in your marriage or maybe you're in a friendship that has become needy, dependent, or toxic. Whatever kind of relationship it is, you just know that you don't *want* to leave.

And so you hold out hope, begging God for change and refinement. Confident enough to set some boundaries but hopeful enough not to cut it totally off.

Obviously I've been there too.

But I've discovered that we should be more concerned with the redemption of our circumstance than the reconciliation of an earthly relationship.

Webster's Dictionary defines redemption as "the act of making something better or more acceptable"[1] while the act of being reconciled is defined as "to restore to friendship or harmony; to settle or resolve."[2]

Let's be very clear on something. I wanted very much to reconcile my relationship with my father. I wanted it to be resolved and settled. There is a still a deep, albeit far-off, hope of that happening. But we don't have to wait on the reconciliation of a relationship, or even a circumstance, to see the redemption of the circumstance.

I want to dive deeper into this thought process because I've spoken with some women who thought redemption would only be found in reconciliation or restoration. For years I waited to even look for redemption until I experienced relationship reconciliation.

But a circumstance does not have to be settled to get better. In fact, we see often in Scripture that God takes something broken and doesn't necessarily put it back together again.

Instead, he makes it new.

THE PASSAGE

For the longest time I sat around waiting for what I thought healing would look like.

Wholeness.

Happiness.

Togetherness.

But I've begun to accept that God never said that he's going to put the broken pieces of my life back together. He never said he'll make things go "back to normal," that he'll make them feel better, or that I'll ever actually feel "whole" again.

Instead, he said, "'Behold, I am making all things new.'" (Revelation 21:5)

Sometimes the broken pieces are broken for a reason. Sometimes God allows the pieces to break so far that they turn into dust so he can take you somewhere

SOMETIMES THE BROKEN PIECES ARE BROKEN FOR A REASON.

you wouldn't have gone had you remained "whole." These are the places where he will earn more glory, more honor, more praise than we could have ever mustered up on our own.

In Isaiah, chapter 43, we read some of the most beautiful words in Scripture.

> But now thus says the Lord, he who created you, O Jacob, he who formed you, O Israel: "Fear not, for I have redeemed you; I have called you by name, you are mine. When you pass through the waters, I will be with you; and through the rivers, they shall not overwhelm you; when you walk through fire you shall not be burned, and the flame shall not consume you."
> (Isaiah 43:1-2)

Let's first put this verse in context because the entire passage begins with "but now," meaning we need to read the previous passage to understand this one.

GOD IS MAKING US BETTER. NOT THE SAME.

In the previous chapter, Isaiah prophesies God's judgment on the Israelites for their stubbornness in their sin. Isaiah asks, "Who gave up Jacob to the looter, and Israel to the plunderers? Was it not the Lord, against whom we have sinned, in whose ways they would not walk, and whose law they would not obey? So he poured on him the heat of his anger and the might of battle . . ." (Isaiah 42:24-25)

I don't want to assume anything, but let's just say God was ticked off. He had delivered Israel from devastation and slavery time and again, asking simply that they would remember him, follow his commandments. But time and again they don't, so he gives them over to their sin.

Now that we know the context, chapter 43 tastes sweeter. Isaiah starts back in and says that God has not only called them by name but redeemed them.

Despite their sin, despite their utter brokenness. He has redeemed them. He has called them by name. They are his, even still.

Does it undo their brokenness and sin? Nope. But there *is* hope.

God is the same for you and me as he was for them. Through the blood of Jesus, we are now all his chosen people, redeemed and called by his name. These beautiful promises, like walking through fire unharmed, are true for us too.

But what if you are walking through the fire right now and, well, you feel a little burnt?

These verses do not promise a peaceful walk through the park. Though God protects them, they still have to walk through the fire.

We'll always have fires to walk through. But when we're walking with God, we will not get burned.

Bad things happen and people fail us. We are stubborn and sinful. But God provides hope of redemption even in the fire.

He is the source of redemption, not the people or circumstances around us.

We must continue to believe that no matter how fierce our fire looks, he can still redeem, even if he doesn't restore. He is making us better, not the same.

THE PIVOT

So what do we do with all of the verses that insinuate — no, actually promise —that if we simply ask, we will receive? What do we do when God says his promises and purposes are good—to prosper and not to harm us—but we're still walking through that fire?

Fast forward a few hundred years and Peter reminds us, "Do not overlook this one fact, beloved, that with the Lord, one day is as a thousand years, and a thousand years is as one day. The Lord is not slow to fulfill his promise as some of you count slowness, but is patient toward you . . ." (2 Peter 3:8-9)

We have to remind ourselves that God operates outside the confines of time. That when we read Scripture we do so with finite minds, only aware of our lifetimes. Sure, conceptually, we understand there are lifetimes before and after us, but our focus is on the here and now—our lifetime.

God's good plan operates outside of our lifetime. The purposes for our hope and future play out under the umbrella of God's ten thousand-foot view.

Peter is talking about Jesus's return in this verse, but we can apply this concept to the redemption we are waiting for right now. The healing, the reconciliation, the fulfillment of God's promises that you are begging for. The rescue from the fire. Rest assured that he is not slow to answer.

We have to remember that God is perfect, and therefore his timing is also perfect. And even while the wait is long, the fire is hot, and we don't understand the goodness that could possibly come from what we're walking through, we can rest assured that God will always be true to his word.

And so we keep watching for redemption regardless of reconciliation. Is it difficult? More like brutal. But I have to choose to believe that God is doing something new here, bringing something better out of the heartache of this relationship. Pivoting from what I feel about my dad to what I know about my Father.

I've often confused the redemption of heartache with the restoration of relationship. And please hear me, friend, we must remember they are not one in the same.

> **WHAT WAS ONCE BROKEN IS NOT MADE WHOLE IN THE RESTORATION BUT IN GOD'S REDEMPTION OF WHO IS BROKEN. US.**

Unfortunately, we have no say in whether a relationship

is restored here on earth. Sure, we should pursue peace as much as possible, but we can never force someone to make things right with us—nor should we want to.

But we do have a choice in whether we see redemption. Not because we hold the power to redeem, but because we surrender to the God who does. We can wallow in our broken relationships, waiting for restoration, or we can let go and allow God to work in and through that same brokenness to bring glory to himself.

What was once broken is not made whole in the restoration but in God's redemption of *who* is broken. Us.

Are you desperate for restoration today? Could it be that what you're craving is actually redemption?

God *can* redeem your circumstance. You don't have to wait for restoration of that relationship or for the fire to subside. It is possible for him to do something better, something new right now. The choice is up to you.

14 | **BELIEVING GOD CHOSE YOU**
when you're rejected in the world

When I share my testimony publicly, people often ask me after what my relationship with my father is like now. I used to say, "Well, it's complicated," because despite everything we had been through, I still wanted a relationship with him.

It's not like he was a coach or a family friend or an uncle. Our relationship wasn't one I could so easily give up on. It was a relationship I had craved so much in my young life that I had unknowingly walked right into the abuse.

What daughter doesn't want to be loved by her father?

Nearly two years after our last communication, Jeff and I got on the same page about my dad. My parents had been divorced for a year, and I hadn't heard from him since that July text I mentioned a few chapters ago. And yet, my heart cried out for him, as did Jeff's. After all, he was still my dad, and he still roamed the earth just thirty miles down the road. I was sick over our lack of relationship.

> **I WAS DESPERATELY TRYING TO HOLD FAST TO WHAT GOD WANTED ME TO DO.**

So we arranged a meeting and on January 2, 2020, Jeff and I sat down with my dad over coffee.

He was late, which was unlike him. As it turned out, he went to the wrong cafe.

"He'll be in here in ten minutes," Jeff said.

I could feel the muscles in my neck and back tense up.

"Have you decided what you want to say to him?" He asked. I shook my head as tears began to form. I still couldn't believe that I was the one who arranged the meeting to make things right with my dad, who did me wrong. Not him.

But I was desperately trying to hold fast to what God wanted me to do. I was trying to forgive and restore a relationship with my father. I was trying to honor my father (and mother). I was doing my best to live at peace with him.

He walked in; I stood and hugged him tightly while completely breaking down. To my surprise, he looked like my dad. Not more or less weary. Not older or younger. Not grayer or wider or skinnier. Just the same. Had two years really gone by?

And then we sat down and got to business.

I asked him all the questions I wanted. I shocked myself with how my business-like I was.

I asked if he had been abused as a child (a question that had haunted me for years and would have honestly been a relief to me).

I asked if he's going to church.

I asked what he's told other people.

I asked why he had never come to me about it, why he had never confessed if he had known it was wrong.

I asked why he didn't have a relationship with any of his old friends. (They were my mom's friends, apparently.)

I asked if he had done this to anyone else.

The answers didn't shock or surprise me, and I felt a bit of a burden lift off my shoulders.

After a few blunt questions, I made it abundantly clear that I was open to rebuilding a relationship with him, but he was going to have to pursue it. That meant that he could contact me and even if I didn't respond, I wanted him to continue reaching out if that's what he really wanted.

That afternoon Jeff and I received emails from him. Once again, they were generic.

> I am sorry all of this happened. As always, I wish I could go back in time . . . but I cannot. I am sorry it

is causing so much hurt to you. I wish there was an easier and less hurtful way to make our way through this. But I have not figured one out.

I am available to you ANYTIME and ANYWHERE for ANYTHING. I will check in with you on a somewhat regular basis. I love both you and Jeff.

I have *never* heard from him again.

I wanted to reach out to him anyway. I wanted to remind him of the deal we had made—that he was supposed to pursue me, remember? He's supposed to *want* a relationship with me. He's the father; I'm the daughter. I'm the victim. His victim.

THE WOUND HAD BEEN SMOOTHED OVER, BUT NOW IT WAS GAPING.

I soon discovered that I was no longer the Becky that I once was. I wasn't the girl who was going to chase after someone who didn't want her in return. I wasn't going to manipulate my way around the boundaries that Jeff and I had drawn for ourselves and for our family. As much as I wanted to.

And y'all, I had a clear issue with the Lord over this.

Jeff and I had felt the Holy Spirit move us to meet with him on that day. We never felt confident about the Spirit's movement at the same time, so when we were finally aligned, we thought something good would come from it.

So my beef with God was something like, "If you knew this was going to happen, and he wasn't going to pursue a relationship with me anyway, then why open the door for it in the first place? Why prompt us to meet with him in the first place?"

The wound had been smoothed over, but now it was gaping. I felt like I was rejected all over again.

One of the definitions of rejection is to "discard as useless or unsatisfactory."[1] Let me just tell you how hard this hits when your father is doing the rejecting.

I spent my teenage years doing everything I could to not be discarded. To be useful. To be satisfactory. I spent many of my waking hours begging for my father's love, his approval, his pride. And when I cut it off, when I had realized what he did and finally said no, I was rejected.

And then years later, when I desperately tried to confront the issue, reassuring him how loved he was, how much I forgave him (which I truly did), how much grace we had for him, and how much we still wanted to reform a relationship with him, I was *still* rejected.

I realized, once again, that now I am of no use to him.

This is what a lot of my counseling sessions are spent on—the idea that the man who is obligated to love, protect, cherish, honor, adore me doesn't. His rejection smashed my self-esteem, and despite my best efforts, I haven't fully recovered. I have been conditioned to attach my usefulness with my value. My ability to perform with my ability to be loved.

Maybe you're there today.

Maybe you've experienced rejection, whether it be from your father, a man, or a friend, and you're wondering what else you have to offer. Maybe you're frustrated that you are even upset about it—knowing that your value comes from the Lord but stinging long after the person has gone.

I wish we were sitting across from each other so I could squeeze your hand and tell you that you are not alone. I wish I could share with you face to face that God has given us so many examples in Scripture of mighty men and women who were rejected and cast out but *still used* and chosen by him.

But since we are not face to face in a gourmet coffee shop somewhere, these words spilled across the page will just have to do.

THE PASSAGE

While there are many stories throughout Scripture of people who were rejected by man, their family, their followers, the one that sticks out to me is the story of Leah.

I have always struggled with this story because it just feels unfair. Yet, I know God has something for us to learn.

The story kicks off with Jacob, one of the heroes of the Old Testament. He's a descendant of Isaac and Rebekah. Jacob was the one who actually "stole" Esau's birthright at the suggestion and prompting of his mother!

After his father, Isaac blessed him and directed him, "'You must not take a wife from the Canaanite women. Arise, go to Paddan-aram to the house of Bethuel your mother's father, and take as your wife from there one of the daughters of Laban your mother's brother.'" (Genesis 28:1-2)

Isaac is asking the same thing of Jacob as his father, Abraham, did to him. Abraham did not allow Isaac to marry from the Canaanites, which is why he sent his servant to find Rebekah in the first place. Jacob must also return to the land of their extended family and find a wife instead of their current territory.

So Jacob traveled to his Uncle Laban's house and found some men in a pasture tending to sheep in the middle of the day. He asked about Laban and if it was well with him. "While he was still speaking with them, Rachel came with her father's sheep, for she was a shepherdess." (Genesis 29:9)

Jacob ran to help her roll the stone from the mouth of the well. "Then Jacob kissed Rachel and wept aloud." (Genesis 29:11) Scholars assume that Rachel was very attractive, and it was nearly "love at first sight." Jacob was also a foreigner in this land and had been traveling for a while, so the love at first sight was likely mixed with some relief.

After a month of employing Jacob, Laban asks what his wages should be. (Genesis 29:15) Between this question and Jacob's answer, we meet Leah.

Laban had two daughters. Leah was the oldest and Rachel, the youngest. "Leah's eyes were weak, but Rachel was beautiful in form and appearance." (Genesis 29:17) The description alone feels unfair but "Jacob loved Rachel."

He offers to work for seven years to marry Rachel. *Seven* years. Can you imagine? He must have loved her very much. It was, of course, not customary to marry off the younger daughter first, but Laban agreed. "So Jacob served seven years for Rachel, and they seemed to him but a few days because of the love he had for her." (Genesis 29:20)

What must it have been like for Leah? A few of my friends from college and high school watched their younger sisters marry before them, and it was not easy for them. There's something slightly backward about it from the get-go since it's often assumed that the older sister would marry first.

And then to know that Jacob could have picked you but instead picked your younger sister? Leah no doubt felt rejected.

Then Leah becomes her father's pawn in a game of deception.

After seven years, Jacob and Rachel are ready to get married. But instead of Rachel under the veil, it was Leah! Oh, the scandal! It sounds like an episode of Days of Our Lives.

Laban switched the women to trick Jacob into marrying Leah first. He blamed the customs of their country—like Jacob should have been aware all along.

Understandably angry, Jacob confronted Laban, who agreed he would hand over Rachel only if Jacob worked for another seven years.

I cannot imagine all of the broken hearts involved here.

Scripture is clear that Jacob loved Rachel more than Leah. It spells it out more than a few times. In fact, Leah says that she is hated.

But because she was unloved by her husband, God gave her children.

This created competition with her sister, because Rachel was not blessed with children. You can read the back and forth in the chapter, but it makes like a classic story of sisters fighting over a man.

Instead of taking the children as a blessing from God, Leah tried to use the children to make Jacob love her. For each child, she hoped her husband would love her.

Though she was loved by God, she kept vying for man's love and attention.

THOUGH SHE WAS LOVED BY GOD, LEAH KEPT VYING FOR MAN'S LOVE AND ATTENTION.

Isn't this what we all do on a regular basis? God has seen us and given us what is *best* for us, and yet we want something else. We want success, human affirmation, blessing, honor, and sometimes even fame. And when we are rejected, do we accept it?

Nope. Instead we try harder.

The competition with children between Leah and Rachel did not stop. Finally, after Leah she named her fourth son Judah, she said, "'This time I will praise the Lord.'" (Genesis

29:35)

She decided her time was better spent praising the Lord than working for Jacob's attention. She accepted her husband's rejection and decided to be happy with her beautiful baby boys.

I've always thought it was kind of the Lord to bring Jesus from the line of Judah. Rachel was the wife that Jacob loved, the one that bore Joseph who made sure an entire generation of people survived a famine.

But hundreds of years later, Jesus, our savior, would come from this moment that Leah, *the rejected one*, praised the Lord.

THE PIVOT

Rejection is going to be a fact of life for all of us. Whether it comes in big or small forms—the rejection of a father, a spouse, a boss, the declined job offer, the invitation that gets lost in the mail, the friend that forgets to call—we will feel its sting at one point.

But this is when we take our eyes off the person who rejected us and put them back on the God who chooses us, just as Leah finally did with Judah.

First Peter 2:9-10 says,

> But you are a chosen race, a royal priesthood, a holy nation, a people for his own possession, that you may proclaim the excellencies of him who called you out

of darkness into his marvelous light. Once you were not a people, but now you are God's people; once you had not received mercy, but now you have received mercy."

You, my friend, are a chosen woman. No matter who has rejected you. No matter whose attention you are seeking and not receiving. No matter what opportunities or relationships have not worked out for you. God chose you, and he is better than any relationship or opportunity or attention that you can seek!

GOD CHOSE YOU, AND HE IS BETTER THAN ANY RELATIONSHIP THAT YOU CAN SEEK.

This might not take the sting away at first, I totally get that. But over time, if you let this truth wash over you enough, it will become a part of who you are. It will be woven into the fabric of your being and then you too will turn from saying "I have been rejected" to "I will praise the Lord."

Focus today on what the Lord has given you, what he's done for you, what he is doing for you. Pivot your attitude from one of rejection to one of receiving. Even if you can only praise God for the breath in your lungs.

There is always something to be thankful for. You are a daughter of the King of Kings! You are his. Forever and always. Literally, nothing can separate you from his love and from his mercy. You are his people.

My prayer for you today is that you pivot from your rejection to your identity in Christ. That somehow, in some way, that would be enough for you. That you can believe God delights in choosing you.

15 | BELIEVING GOD IS WITH YOU
when you feel all alone

Author's Note: *This chapter could be triggering to some, as it includes brief details of a forensic interview with the police.*

Six weeks after Jeff and I met with my father for breakfast that cold January morning, life drastically changed once again. You would think I'd be used to it by now.

It was a Monday holiday and the kids were home from school. I wanted to be a fun mom and took the kids to at an arcade in the next town over. We played games and ate lunch, I beat my boys in Super Mario Kart, and I got a high score on the pinball machine.

Out of the blue on our way home from the arcade, one of the kids asked me about my father. They would do this on occasion, asking where he was or if he still has a car (my oldest's favorite question). I often remind myself that not only did I lose a father, but they lost a grandfather too. And for their little, young, innocent minds to comprehend the gravity of what had taken place was overwhelming and heartbreaking.

I HAD SPENT THE LAST TWO YEARS CONVINCING MYSELF THAT I WAS THE ONLY ONE.

I can't remember what question they asked me, but it had me thinking about him, my trauma, my parents for the rest of the afternoon and evening. We ate pizza for dinner and attempted an early bedtime. This mama was worn out by the fun of the day.

But in the moments that followed bedtime, new information was revealed to Jeff and I about my father, indicating that his past was not as "past" as we thought. I was horrified and shattered. Jeff was furious. We were crushed.

And as difficult as this might be for you to believe, I was also *shocked*. I had spent thirty years convincing myself that this was not who my father was, just something that he had done. And, I had spent the last two years convincing myself that I was the only one.

But that was no longer true.

My brother-in-law came over to our house and drove Jeff to meet my brother and Jeff's dad. They were taking charge. We would pursue justice not only relationally but criminally.

I had never dreamt that it would come to this point.

A few days later I talked with a friend who runs the local child advocacy center. He graciously walked me through all my options in legally "coming forward." He listened to me as I cried and cried with me as I yelled. We knew we needed to go to the police.

People have asked me why I didn't go straight to the police when I worked with my counselor. I have shamed myself for not reporting my dad when I was a child. But the truth is that I wasn't ready. I wasn't strong enough. I would have crumbled if God had not been preparing me for this day.

Also, it's important for you to know I have found that there's no blessing in going *backward*. Of course, I can learn lessons and work through thoughts. But to wonder *what if* or *why not* has brought nothing but more pain into my heart, so I try not to go there.

And either way, we were here now. Armed with new information that was forcing us to come forward with old information.

The Monday of spring break, Jeff and I walked into the local police station to meet with a detective. He made me aware of my options based on the dates and places things occurred and explained what the process would look like. The detective was kind, and I was thankful he was also a believer. I sat on the couch in tears, squeezing my husband's hand as I took it all in. It was a surreal experience.

A few days later, I came back all on my own. I walked into an interview room with the same detective, camera rolling. I knew what was coming.

He asked me to describe, in detail, what happened to me. I explained the specifics of the rooms we were in, situations I was put in, the timeline surrounding the abuse, and of the physical parts of my trauma.

> **SUFFERING ITSELF IS LONELY, BUT BEING PHYSICALLY ALONE WHILE SUFFERING IS EXCRUCIATING.**

At one point the detective noticed an emerging pattern about how the abuse began each time. It hit me like a crashing wave hits the sand before returning to the sea. I realized my father used me every chance he got. He created chances to use me. He even created an environment where I was obligated to give him chances to use me.

I shook my head. I remember saying, "This is so messed up." And it was. I mean, it *is*.

What felt like hours later, I nervously thanked the detective for his time and climbed into my car and cried like I hadn't cried before. I felt so incredibly alone.

My family and friends had been wonderfully supportive in the months and weeks leading up to the interview. They prayed over me and encouraged me the best they could. But at the end of the day, I had to walk into that interview alone. I had to recount all the details again and again by myself. And I hold the memories so vividly in my mind and heart that they wear me down on a daily basis.

Sometimes we have to walk through our suffering without people. Suffering itself is lonely, but being physically alone while suffering is excruciating. But when I was sitting in that bleak interview room with only a detective, a camera, and my memories, I reminded myself that God was with me.

Yes, I had to suffer my abuse alone. *But God was with me.*

Yes, I had to walk into that counselor's office in 2018 alone. *But God was with me.*

Yes, I had to walk through the forensic interview alone. *But God was with me.*

God is with you in whatever season of suffering or solitude you're walking through too.

It's hard to understand God being with you while something terrible is happening—a miscarriage, betrayal, abuse, death. But he tells us in his Word he is there even still.

THE PASSAGE

In the book of Genesis, a man named Joseph was sold into slavery, falsely accused, and forgotten by everyone important in his life. If there was anyone ever in Scripture who felt alone, it must be him. And yet the Bible emphasizes that "God was with Joseph" in every season.

When we meet up with Joseph for the first time, this is what we know:

- He is the beloved (and favorite) son of Jacob and Rachel, the wife that Jacob loved.
- He is a seventeen-year-old shepherd boy.
- His dad made him a special coat.
- His brothers hated him.

When I read the story at first glance, I honestly understood why.

Joseph was the tattle-tale know-it-all daddy's favorite son, and he wasn't at all oblivious to it. He knew it.

And to make matters more intense, he had dreams of his family bowing down to him, making them hate him even more. In fact, Scripture tells us that even "his father rebuked him and said to him, 'What is this dream that you have dreamed? Shall I and your mother and your brothers indeed come to bow ourselves to the ground before you?'" (Genesis 37:10)

Are you starting to get it yet?

One afternoon, Jacob asks Joseph to check on his brothers, but he doesn't find them in the field where they're supposed to be. So, after Joseph receives some friendly directions from a neighbor, he heads into the next town over to find them.

Scripture says, "They saw him from afar, and before he

came near to them, they conspired against him to kill him." (Genesis 37:18)

I guess you could say that escalated quickly.

Fortunately for Joseph, he has at least one brother who is willing to stand up for him and not kill him. He suggests something a tad lighter instead—that they throw him into the bottom of a pit with no water. So that's what they do and leave him.

Afterward, the brothers see a caravan, assumed to be gypsies, coming up their road. They grab Joseph out of the pit and sell him to these strangers. Sounds like those dreams of everyone bowing down to him were definitely working out for him.

JOSEPH HAD DONE NOTHING TO DESERVE THIS KIND OF TREATMENT FROM HIS FAMILY.

So, besides being a tattle-tale and maybe a bit spoiled (my words not Scripture's), he had done nothing wrong— nothing to deserve this kind of treatment from his family.

Of course, I completely identify with this and perhaps you do too. Perhaps you've be cheated or wronged, betrayed or abandoned by someone who was supposed to be your ride or die kind of person. I hope you see by the end of this story that you are not the only one.

After Joseph is sold into slavery to the gypsies, several

things happen.

First, he is sold to Potiphar, an officer of Pharaoh in Egypt. Joseph serves Potiphar loyally. Scripture tells us,

> The Lord was with Joseph, and he became a successful man, and he was in the house of his Egyptian master. His master saw that the Lord was with him and that the Lord caused all that he did to succeed in his hands. So Joseph found favor in his sight and attended him, and he made him the overseer of his house and put him in charge of all that he had. (Genesis 39:2-4)

Things were looking up for Joseph. God was with him. He was successful—even as a servant. The Lord even blessed the Egyptians for the sake of Joseph, which seems only "fair" after what had happened to him.

Or so you might think.

Soon after his success, Joseph had another problem. Potiphar's wife, well, she wanted him. Instead of giving in to the temptation, Joseph "left his garment in her hand and fled and got out of the house." (Genesis 39:12)

I can only imagine Potiphar's wife was embarrassed by the rejection of her husband's servant. So she took Joseph's garment and "called to the men of her household and said to them, 'See he has brought among us a Hebrew to laugh at us. He came in to me to lie with me and I cried out with a loud voice.'" (Genesis 39:14)

We know that wasn't true but seeing as she was holding

Joseph's garment in her hand, Potiphar believed her and threw Joseph in the worst jail.

Again, unfairly treated.

Again, thrown into a pit that was undeserved.

And yet again, "the Lord was with Joseph and showed him steadfast love and gave him favor in the sight of the keeper of the prison." (Genesis 39:21)

I can't presume to know what you're thinking after reading all of that, but if I were Joseph, I would be confused. I would ask God what I was doing wrong. I would be angry and upset, to say the very least. And yet, even in these terrible and unjust circumstances, God's Word is repeatedly clear—he was with Joseph.

In the pit.

In Pharoah's house.

In the prison.

And I can't help but relate. I wondered where God was when I was suffering at the hands of my father. I wondered where God was when I begged for true repentance. I wondered where God was when I described my abuse in the coldness of a police station.

But could it be that all along, he was right there with me? Could it be that while allowing the broken things, he was preparing a way of righteousness and glory for himself?

This is what I will choose to believe. This is what I *have* to believe after reading Joseph's story, after living my own. He is consistently with me, even when I feel all alone.

And he is with *you* too.

I imagine you've found yourself in less than ideal circumstances at one point or another. Whether it's a consequence of your own making or consequences of living in a fallen world, you can still end up feeling lonely in those moments. The enemy would love nothing more than for you to stay stuck in that loneliness.

> **GOD WILL NEVER ABANDON YOU. NOT IN THE PRISON, NOT IN THE POLICE STATION.**

Instead, my prayer for you is that you would understand this one thing: God is with you.

When the Israelites were wandering through the wilderness, Moses says, "The Lord your God has blessed you in all the work of your hands. He knows your going through this great wilderness. These forty years the Lord your God has been with you. You have lacked nothing." (Deuteronomy 2:7)

When Jesus ascended into heaven, he left the earth saying, "'And behold, I am with you always, to the end of the age.'" (Matthew 28:20)

I could have left the police station that day overcome with sadness. I mean, it was a sad day doing a sad thing. But instead, I deliberately chose to believe what I know about God.

I chose to believe that no matter where I went or what I had to do, God was with me. I chose to remember all of the times he was with me before. I chose to remember that he is faithful, good, kind, and compassionate and even in the prison—or police station—he is there.

God will never abandon you. Not while sitting in the prison, not while waiting in the police station. Not in the hospital, not in the funeral home, not in the crisis pregnancy center.

This is a most pivotal truth for each of us—making the shift from feeling alone to knowing we're not. The God that was with Joseph, with the Israelites, with the disciples, is the same God who still shows up, who is with you today in this moment, even now as you're reading.

Don't drown in your loneliness, friend. Trust God's continued promise that he will be with you. Believe him to be the very God that he says he is over and again in Scripture. And believe him to be that God for you.

REJOICE NOT OVER ME, O MY ENEMY; WHEN I FALL, I SHALL RISE; WHEN I SIT IN DARKNESS, THE LORD WILL BE A LIGHT TO ME.

micah 7:8

16 | **BELIEVING GOD IS JUST**
and that's better than your own revenge

I got back in my car and pulled down the visor mirror. I looked exactly as I expected—makeup halfway down my face, mascara smeared under my eyes, somewhat artfully I might add. I'd just finished meeting with the prosecutor's office in my legal case and, for lack of better words, it was awful. I couldn't believe this was my life. No, that this is my life.

A Grand Jury had found there was sufficient evidence to indict and make a subsequent arrest. I never wanted it to come to this. Never dreamt of prosecuting my own father, no matter how awful he treated me. I struggled with the decision to move forward legally. I lost sleep over it, I got physically sick over it, and I argued with God over it.

But ultimately, for reasons that are not mine to share,

this was the right decision for our family, even if we hated it.

And listen, I *want* God's will to be done but not like this. Maybe you've felt that way before, finding the tension between trusting that God wants what's best but standing convinced this can't possibly be it.

> **I WANT GOD'S WILL TO BE DONE, BUT NOT LIKE THIS.**

I hate walking through details of my abuse repeatedly. I hate feeling like no one is listening, but everyone is watching me, judging me, criticizing me.

Will she crumble under the pressure?

Will her efforts fail?

Will she give in or stay strong?

I hate feeling exposed and vulnerable even if it is only supposed to be "one more time." And I hate, beyond all that is wrong in this world, that this doesn't feel like it's going to be justice at all.

Let me be downright honest with you about this prosecutor meeting. I prepared for this day for over a year. I knew what I wanted, what justice would feel like for me, and I was ready to fight for it. I had waited for it, cried over it, and prayed over it, but I had also practiced yelling over it. I imagined myself as Jack Nicholson in A Few Good Men, shouting "You can't handle the truth!"

I had spent most of my life protecting everyone else, but now I felt strong enough to fight for myself, and it was important for me to do so. I was ready to walk into that office and in a slightly more lady-like version of Erin Brockovich, slam my fists on the conference table and shout, "This is unacceptable, and I will not accept any less than what I deserve."

But instead of a courtroom or a conference table filled with attorneys, I sat in a somber meeting room in front of a small but brave group of people who graciously decided to serve me—serve our community—and cried my guts out. Because, despite my now somewhat buried hope of reconciliation with my father, I wanted justice at all costs.

Not out of vengeance or spite or anger but out of a deep desire to do all I can in making it right.

And when it comes down to it, it doesn't feel fair that my father gets to go about his life as if nothing happened, without a shred of remorse or repentance while I remain haunted by his abuse every single day.

It doesn't feel right that this man who touted God and the gospel for the better part of thirty-six years, this man who led me to my own personal relationship with Jesus, would continue to sing in a choir without so much as an attempt at taking responsibility for all he has done wrong.

So yeah, you better believe that for a million reasons and in a million ways, I wanted justice.

Maybe you're in a similar situation that involves an ongoing legal battle. Maybe you're begging God for justice and you're certain it looks a specific way.

But even if you aren't, the news shows us countless ways

that evildoers evade justice. People commit heinous crimes and are let go with a simple slap on the wrist. Or people get away with racial inequity or total destruction.

Every day we see injustice go unpunished. We can often wonder where God is in this. I have asked the Lord many times over, "How could you let this happen and not *fix* it?" I've wondered how he's letting something continue, how someone gets off so easy, how people literally seem to get away with murder.

But what if God's idea of justice doesn't resemble our own?

What if my dad is never proven guilty or never forced to take ownership? What if we never get justice here on earth? How can we ever reconcile that?

If I hear, "Vengeance is the Lord's" one more time I really might scream, but the stone-cold truth is this: it is. And as angry, disappointed, and brokenhearted I am at the unfairness of it all, I again come to the pivot.

In Romans 12, Paul spells out what it looks like follow Christ. He gives this speech about not being conformed to the world and letting your love be genuine and mighty. He tells us to bless those who persecute us and love our enemies.

It's all abstract and general until he sticks a stake in the ground and says, "Beloved, never avenge yourselves, but leave it to the wrath of God, for it is written, 'Vengeance is mine, I will repay, says the Lord.'" (Romans 12:19)

I have wrestled with this hard over the past several years. Vengeance does not mean seeking justice legally. It also doesn't mean *not* seeking justice legally. It also doesn't mean that we should stay silent, even if the truth might hurt someone else.

In fact, Matthew Henry's Complete Commentary says, "When anybody has done you any ill turn, do not desire nor endeavor to bring the like mischief or inconvenience upon him. It is not forbidden to the magistrate to do justice to those that are wronged . . . but it forbids private revenge, which flows from anger and ill-will."[1]

WE CAN SEEK EARTHLY JUSTICE, BUT THE MANNER IN WHICH WE SEEK THAT JUSTICE MATTERS.

Make no mistake, we can seek earthly justice, but the manner in which we seek that justice *matters*. Are we doing it out of revenge, to make them hurt like they hurt us? Or are we trying to make things right, legally or spiritually?

Maybe you've been left, wronged, betrayed, taken advantage of, and all you see is a smile on their face while the heartbreak consumes you. You think, "Why do they get to move on with their lives while I sit in the mess they made? Why do they have a fresh start and a clean slate when all I'm left with is broken pieces?"

I see you, friend, and I want you to know you are not alone. I know it doesn't *feel* good and often it doesn't feel fair. But if we aren't careful, we can drown believing the lies that God loves them and not me, or God doesn't care about what happened to me.

Like I said to the prosecutor that rainy April morning, "This isn't fair." He nodded my direction and said, "You're right, it's not. I will never tell you any of this is fair."

And though we see a lot of happy endings in Scripture, we have to admit that hindsight is 20/20. It's easier to see the happy endings when we aren't the ones living through the hard parts. We can see how it all works out, how years and perhaps generations later, God serves up justice for that family or that kingdom.

But while we are smack dab in the middle of it, it's a lot more complicated to turn our other cheek.

THE PASSAGE

As I was praying about what to include in this chapter, I had a difficult time nailing down what this looks like in Scripture. We see a lot of cries for justice, but also a lot of God's mercy extended. We see the enemies of Israel, David, and Solomon overthrown and the wicked destroyed, but we also see the Israelites, God's own people, judged for their sin too.

It serves as a not so subtle reminder that not one of us is beyond God's judgment, but thankfully not beyond his mercy. What I see throughout Scripture is that God holds mercy and grace in the same hands he holds truth and justice. It's never either/or, only both/and.

So what does that mean? Does that mean I should call it a day and let God exercise his own justice (or mercy) on my father? Does it mean you should stand down and not pursue retribution for the ways that you've been wronged?

Let's take a deeper look.

Isaiah 61 is one of my favorites on this subject.

> The Spirit of the Lord God is upon me, because the Lord has anointed me to bring good news to the poor, he has sent me to bind up the brokenhearted, to proclaim liberty to the captives, and the opening of the prison to those who are bound; to proclaim the year of the Lord's favor, and the day of vengeance of our God; to comfort all who mourn; to grant to those who mourn in Zion—to give them a beautiful headdress instead of ashes, the oil of gladness instead of mourning, the garment of praise instead of a faint spirit; that they may be called oaks of righteousness, the planting of the Lord, that he may be glorified. They shall build up the ancient ruins; they shall raise up the former devastations; they shall repair the ruined cities, the devastations of many generations. (Isaiah 61:1-4)

The day of vengeance Isaiah prophesies here is in the future, when God returns to the earth. It's a day beyond here, beyond us and our generation.

Judgment day is coming for *all* of us. The day when the Lord's favor will forever be upon us—on you and me—and we will be released from the justice *he could have* bestowed on us. The day is also coming when his wrath will be released on those who don't believe.

We can do our part to seek justice for ourselves, legally and even spiritually. But the rest, we have to leave up to the Lord. We have to acknowledge that we might not see, experience, or even feel earthly justice. We might not see the person who wronged us suffer the consequence of their sin, but we can believe that there *are* consequences to their sin. Just as there are consequences to our own.

THE BOTTOM LINE IS THAT WE CAN FIGHT FOR JUSTICE WITHOUT FIXATING ON JUSTICE.

Paul writes in his letter to the Galatians, "Do not be deceived: God is not mocked, for whatever one sows, that will he also reap. For the one who sows to his own flesh will from the flesh reap corruption, but the one who sows to the Spirit will from the Spirit reap eternal life." Galatians 6:7-8

I have to believe that even if my father is a Christian and ends up in heaven, he will suffer consequences of his sin on earth, and that he will indeed reap what he has sown, regardless of earthly justice. I have to believe that God knows what he's doing better than I know what I'm doing.

That God has my best interest at heart, and honestly, he also has my dad's.

Does it always *feel* fair? Absolutely not.

Back in Isaiah 61, he continues, "For I the Lord love justice; I hate robbery and wrong; I will faithfully give them their recompense and I will make an everlasting covenant with them." (Isaiah 61:8)

This is what we have to believe—that the Lord, with all of his mercy, also loves justice. We have to pivot from our hurt feelings, hurt egos, hurt bodies, hurt pocketbooks to trust in a God who is both grace and truth.

Does this make it easier for you to *not* see justice? Nope.

Does it help your feelings when you see an enemy, like a real enemy, succeeding while you're floundering? Nope.

The bottom line is that we can fight for justice without fixating on justice. We can pursue what's right while also pursuing WHO is right. When we shift our focus from what feels and seems fair back to the unfairness of the entire gospel, we can see not only our enemies from God's perspective but ourselves. If the gospel was fair, we would all go to hell.

And I don't know about you, but when I view myself from that ten thousand-foot view that God views me with, and I see all the wrong that I have done that has been forgiven, and I know who God is and says that he will always be, I can believe that he is working it all out in his timing and in his way.

When I pivot my focus from earthly justice to heavenly

justice, I have no other choice than to release control over the situation. I can do my part and then be at peace with leaving the rest up to God.

At this point, I have received no earthly justice. And maybe I never will. It stings, and there are days I feel I can't live with it. Some days I get angry with the Lord for not only allowing it to happen but then not fixing it.

But often, when I choose to believe his justice is better than my revenge, I live at peace even in the waiting, even in the injustice of it all. I live at peace because I know that my God is for and with me and is working all things together for my good and his glory.

Even if I *never* see justice on this earth.

PART THREE

GOD IS OUR REFUGE & STRENGTH, A VERY PRESENT HELP IN TROUBLE.

psalm 46:1

17 | LORD, I BELIEVE, HELP MY UNBELIEF

During the months I spent hammering out the words of this book, a few things happened. First, my father was arrested, bonded out, and offered a plea that he has spent the better part of my writing time negotiating. It has been a roller coaster of emotions.

We also lost one of our closest friends. We prayed and begged God to heal him this side of heaven. But he didn't. The world lost a strong, godly man. We lost a friend. And his wife, Sarah, lost a husband and the father of her girls. A *wonderful* father.

And then the Lord has said several no's to me lately. Dreams dashed, waiting extended, relationships severed, and my heart left broken again and again.

To be honest, I wanted to scrap this book. I wanted to

hold the delete button down from the bottom to the top. I thought, *This is not a story I can tell now.* Certainly this is not a message God would have me preach. This call to believe is certainly not what's in my heart now.

> **HERE I AM ENCOURAGING YOU TO CHOOSE BELIEF WHILE I STILL STRUGGLE TO BELIEVE.**

I'm hurting, I'm broken, I'm disappointed, and I'm angry.

Yet, God would not relent.

He reminded me about my purpose in the beginning of these pages, when I mentioned many books like this are written after the answered prayer. I stressed how important it was for me to write this in the middle of my unanswered prayers. But I did not anticipate the difficulties that would lie ahead.

And so here I am months after beginning to write about believing God when we don't want to, months after encouraging you to choose belief, choose belief, choose belief, while I still struggle to believe.

And as I sat in my doubt, my struggle, and my hurt, I had this thought: *Maybe this is the whole point.* God isn't upset with the struggling, he's not upset with me and he's not upset with you. He isn't chastising us or shaming us. He's not even angry. Instead, he is simply and patiently waiting with me . . . pursuing me, loving me, and guiding me through my heartache.

The day after we celebrated my friend, Dan's life, I

was scheduled to speak at a women's conference the next state over. I debated if I would even be up to traveling on an airplane immediately after a memorial service, let alone be able to articulate a message. Again, God made it very clear I was to go.

So I flew to Amarillo and stayed in a quiet hotel room by myself with my thoughts. I cried myself to sleep that night, alone and sad, crying out to God, asking him why he takes the righteous and leaves the wicked. Angry and confused, I poured my heart out and told him exactly what I thought of the situation—and let me tell you, it was not the most holy of conversations.

The next morning, I got up while it was still dark and drove an hour and a half over to Clovis, New Mexico to meet my new friends at Central Baptist Church. I took many deep breaths and prayed many deep prayers in my tiny, bright blue rental car. I walked in the building to smiles and hugs.

I talked about friendship and community.

I talked about serving one another and being a good neighbor.

I talked about God having plans for your life no matter what your circumstances are or were.

But mostly, I talked about Jesus and how much he loves you, despite how it might feel right now, and that he is most worthy of our trust and belief.

I prayed the closing prayer and walked off the stage. We sang one more song and I found myself weeping. I was surprised to find that the tears were not out of my immense grief but instead out of an overwhelming, supernatural sense of peace and contentment despite it. These tears came from knowing God is always who he says he is. I have nothing to offer apart from him.

It was a moment when I acknowledged once again that Jesus is real. The Jesus that I preach day in and day out, the Jesus I serve and know and love, the Jesus that I doubted and questioned and was angry with, he is real. And not only is Jesus real, but his love for me (and you) is also.

The conclusion that I have come to now is this:

I will forever struggle in the balance of belief and doubt.

I will forever ask the Lord to show himself as real in my life.

I will forever wonder why God took my friend so early, why he allows the trauma in my life and the life of others.

And if you've made it this far throughout the pages, my guess is that you, in some small way, are still struggling with these thoughts too, even when you're trying your hardest to keep them at bay.

The point of these last few pages, these final paragraphs in this book, is to encourage you to keep going. To tell you that no matter where you're at today in your heartache, you are in good company. This struggle is not a surprise to the Lord, nor is it a sin.

In Mark chapter 9, we read about a desperate father coming to the disciples for help.

Jesus was returning from a literal mountaintop experience with his closest disciples Peter, James, and John, where he revealed his divinity to them in what we now call the transfiguration. Still riding off the exhilarating experience, they came back down into town to find the rest of the disciples arguing with some scribes over their inability to exorcise a demon from a boy.

Jesus asks, "'What are you arguing about with them?'" (Mark 9:16)

Then, "someone from the crowd answered him, 'Teacher, I brought my son to you, for he has a spirit that makes him mute. And whenever it seizes him, it throws him down, and he foams and grinds his teeth and becomes rigid. So I asked your disciples to cast it out, and they were not able.'" (Mark 9:17-18)

I cannot fathom this father's desperation to heal his son. Later on, we find out that this demon had possessed him since childhood and would "often cast him into fire and into water, to destroy him." (Mark 9:22)

This father was at the end of his rope and all he wanted was healing for his son. He loved his son and was willing to try anything. Maybe, just maybe, this Jesus who he had heard worked miracles, would be the answer.

Putting myself in his shoes, I can't wrap my mind around his heartache. This father had no control over the situation as the demons tried to kill him. His child wasn't throwing a temper tantrum and he couldn't be cured. This father had no way to help his son.

Maybe, in a similar fashion, you find yourself desperate for Jesus's intervention in your pain. Maybe you've been desperate for a while, or maybe you've been desperate for a minute. Maybe you've tried everything humanly possible to fix it, heal it, change it. Maybe you're crying out for answers or crying out in terror. Maybe you, too, have no means to help your situation.

> ## THE BEAUTIFUL THING ABOUT DESPERATION IS THAT JESUS MEETS US THERE.

The beautiful thing about desperation is that Jesus meets us there. We aren't refined in moments of comfort but in these desperate moments when our only hope is found by reaching out to Jesus. Just as he does with this precious father.

When Jesus learns of his plea and that the disciples were unable to cast the demon out, he responds, "'O faithless generation, how long am I to be with you? How long am I to bear with you? Bring [the son] to me.'" (Mark 9:19)

There are two schools of thought on this statement. Some believe Jesus was talking to the disciples, rebuking them for not using the power given to them. Others believe he was addressing the scribes who reveled in the disciples' weakness.

Regardless, Jesus then gently asks the father how long his child has suffered. The father explains his son's condition and pleas with Jesus, "If you can do anything, have compassion on us and help us." (Mark 9:22)

This is the most important part of this passage—or at least it is for me. I see the same internal struggle warring in my mind every day. My prayers often go something like this: "God, I know you can heal this relationship, so would you heal it? But you know, if you don't that's cool too. But does that mean you want me to *do* something about it? Or have I done something wrong if you don't heal it? I know you can do it. I *know* you can. But you know, it's okay if you don't. Maybe you won't. But *please* heal it, God."

Whew.

Can you relate to that at all?

I believe God can do it. I know he can do it. I know he can perform miracles because not only have I heard him doing them, like this father had, but I have seen them with my own eyes. Sure, I haven't seen someone raised from the dead, but I've seen hearts healed and relationships mended. I've seen families be supernaturally provided for, and I've seen unexplained medical healing. I've even encountered what I consider to be an angel or two along the way.

The human part of me doubts whether he will show up and do it again. The human part of me doubts whether he loves me enough to give me what I want. The human part of me finds it easier to expect disappointment.

But God.

God wants us to come to him with the desires of our hearts. God wants us to lay it all out there for him. He wants us to trust him to do it—knowing that we struggle to believe he will. Watch what happens with this father and his son.

"Jesus said to him, "'If you can!' All things are possible for the one who believes.' Immediately the father of the child cried out and said, 'I believe; help my unbelief!'" (Mark 9:23-24)

I believe; help my unbelief.

I want to note two things here. First, this father was honest with Jesus. He did believe that Jesus could perform the miracle. If he didn't, he would not have traveled from far away to see him and his disciples. We also must remember that he had apparently asked the disciples first. They had tried to cast out the demon but couldn't. So any resemblance of doubt could be—dare I say—understandable?

The second thing is that he asks for Jesus's help to believe. What a picture of grace and humanity all in the same sentence. This father believes Jesus and wants to believe him even more. It's not that he is unsure, but he admits his humanity in this plea for help with belief.

This is how we should approach the throne with our belief *and* unbelief. "God, I believe you can do this, but help my unbelief."

Jesus did not shame this father but instead healed his son. He commanded the demon to come out and it did—

he was healed. In this short but powerful moment, Jesus physically demonstrated that all things are possible for those who believe.

But how can *all* things be possible when he doesn't give us so many good, holy, righteous things we ask for— even for those of us who believe?

When I am honest (which, I think we can agree, is a lot of the time), I have to admit that I ask God often, "Do I just not believe enough?" There are so many dark moments, some in the middle of the night, when I cry out to the Lord and beg him to show me the places I don't believe.

Why?

To get what I want.

And that's *so* not the point. The point of belief is not to get what we want but to believe more that God is God.

What we learned from the story of this father is that he was willing to throw himself at the mercy of Jesus. He said, "IF you can help us." That wasn't doubt creeping in, but a realization that Jesus had a plan that might have looked different than his.

There's a difference between mercy and grace, even though often we use them interchangeably. Mercy is when we, the sinner, do *not* get what we deserve. For example, we all deserve hell, but God, through Jesus, has chosen to spare us from that.

On the contrary, grace is *getting* what we do *not* deserve. Like this son being healed, and the father seeing his son healed. That is grace.

Everything above and beyond not receiving an eternal sentence of damnation to hell is God's grace on our lives.

> **JOB REMINDS US, BOTH THE BLESSING AND THE BROKENNESS ARE WITHIN GOD'S SOVEREIGNTY.**

So anything I am believing God to do or give me is extra. That means healing, housing, health, wholeness. It's all extra.

So when God tells us to believe, he wants us to believe in him, not for something other than him. This type of belief acknowledges that he is faithful, kind, good, gracious, merciful, loving, just, that he is sovereign and his ways are higher than ours. We are also believing that his plans are to prosper us and not to harm us, with eternity in mind.

If you ever want to understand suffering, read the book of Job. This poor man lost everything. And his wife tells him to "'curse God and die.'" His response? "'Shall we receive good from God, and shall we not receive evil?'" (Job 2:9, 10)

How much easier it is to accept the blessings of the world as evidence of God's love while accepting the brokenness of the world as evidence lack thereof? Job reminds us, both the blessing and the brokenness are within God's sovereignty. Neither proving or disproving his love for us.

As we know from Job, the enemy had to ask permission to test Job. He has limits, even with you and me. Contrary to popular belief, the Bible never explicitly says, "God will never give you what you can't handle." However it does tell us that the enemy is held within the Lord's parameters.

That's a comforting truth to hold on to when we are suffering and struggling to believe.

No matter his suffering, no matter how angry and bitter Job gets with his circumstance, he always believed God was in control.

Job maintained belief while he suffered by staying focused on the character of God.

And that's what we have to do. Even *while* we still suffer here on earth, we have to focus on what we know to be true of God. We have to continue to pivot from what we feel to what we know. Regardless of our circumstance, of our heartache, of our grief.

We are still mourning the loss of our friend. In fact, just the other night as we got in bed, Jeff leaned over and said, "I really miss Dan today." And we all do. Every day.

But Dan would want us to choose belief. Belief that God has good plans for us while we are still here, belief that God is with us even if he's not, and belief that we will, one day soon, be together again for all eternity.

18 | WHEN WE DOUBT

Here's the deal: God doesn't expect us to have this belief thing down. We know this because we see evidence of his patience in Scripture when people doubt. Doubt isn't the problem; sinning in that doubt is. Like when Abram and Sarai doubted God's promise and he went to Hagar instead.

So what should we do when (not if) we doubt to avoid sin?

First, we need to ask God for help like the father in Mark 9 did.

Start by asking God to show you the places where you struggle to believe. Is it a certain attribute of God that you can't see right now? Is it a prayer you feel like has gone unanswered? Is it that you just don't feel his presence in the moment?

I am not your Holy Spirit and could never pretend to know what is going on in your heart and home right now, but typically I have found that when I am struggling to believe God, it's because I'm far from him. Either I've stopped pursuing him personally, I've been away from church for too long, or I need accountability.

If God reveals this to be the case in your life too, it's simple to start pursuing him again. He's right where he was when you left. He hasn't moved and his Word has not changed. Just start. Now. Grab your Bible and open it up to the Psalms. Start reading about his faithfulness and loving-kindness. Soak it in as much as you possibly can. Understanding who God is will go a long way in helping your doubt.

GOD HASN'T MOVED AND HIS WORD HAS NOT CHANGED.

After you ask God for help in your unbelief, spend time thinking about your last encounter with the Lord. When was the last time you sensed his Spirit move? When was the last time you felt him direct you or lead you to an assignment or a person? What did he asked you to do? Where was he was leading you? Are you still doing that thing? Have you followed the call?

One of the best Bible studies I have ever done is "Experiencing God" by Henry Blackaby.[1] In it, he breaks down how to know and do the will of God. If you are confused or searching in the slightest, I highly suggest this study, but be prepared—though accessible, it's also intense.

> ASSIGNMENTS AREN'T ALL ENCOMPASSING, NOR ARE THEY MUTUALLY EXCLUSIVE.

He suggests that if you find yourself wondering what God has for you next, you should remember what he had for you last and continue to do that very thing until you know what God has for you next.

In terms of doubting God—whether we are doubting his character, his plan, or our own identity in light of his truth—this practice reminds us that God has indeed moved in our lives before.

Maybe you haven't heard a "voice" come from the heavens. Maybe you're unsure of when or if God has ever called you to an assignment. If that's the case let me ask you a few questions:

- Are you married? Your assignment is to be a godly wife and partner to your spouse.
- Are you a mom? Your assignment is to be a godly mom to your kids, whether little or grown.
- Do you have a job? Your assignment is to "work at it with all your heart, as working for the Lord." (Colossians 3:23, NIV)
- Do you have friends? Your assignment is to show

up for them, loving them as Christ loves.

- Do you have a church? Your assignment is to participate and serve.

Assignments are not all-encompassing, nor are they mutually exclusive. God gives us responsibilities, even though he doesn't yell them from the heavens. When he hands these responsibilities to us, he is trusting us with the assignment.

So if you are doubting or even just waiting on God to do the next thing or show you the next way, make sure you are doing the last thing he has given you to do—and do it well.

This leads me into the next thing we can do when we doubt—and that is to remember God's specific faithfulness to us.

Every time I doubt the Lord, the focus tends to be on *me* and not *him*. I am either waiting on him to give me what I'm asking for, or asking him why he has said no.

But if I stop my begging for just a second and turn from my honest (and valid) heartbreak back to who God is, I can remember all the ways he has been overtly faithful to me. If I know (and believe) that the character of God never ever changes, I can conclude he will continue to be faithful to me forever.

So, when we doubt, what do we do? We ask God for help, seek him, obey the last thing he has told us to do, and remember his faithfulness. Ultimately, when it's all boiled down to it, we *choose* to believe.

I know this sounds redundant here because this entire book is about the choice to believe, but if you would be so kind to go with me here for just one more second. If we return to the story of the father who was desperate for his son's healing, we notice the last thing he said to Jesus: "I believe; help my unbelief."

He was choosing to believe, in the middle of unbelief, and that is what God would like us to do too.

> When we doubt his faithfulness, we instead say, "I believe you are faithful."
>
> When we doubt his goodness, we instead say, "I believe you are good."
>
> When we doubt his plans and purposes for our life, we instead say, "I believe your plans are for me and not against me."

It doesn't have to be perfect, and it can come with the follow-up plea for help as the father's did. But it is a choice. I know I might sound like a broken record, but you have a choice today whether you will believe the Lord. You can say, even if you have to say it out loud like I do sometimes, "I believe you, God, not my circumstances. I believe you, God, not my bank account. I believe you, God, not my father." It's your choice but I hope you'll make it today.

19 | BELIEVING DOUBT VS. UNBELIEVING DOUBT

There are two kinds of doubt: believing doubt and unbelieving doubt.

The father in Mark 9 had a believing doubt. His doubt pressed him *into* Christ, not *away* from him. His doubt caused him to reach out to Jesus for help, not run away to find help elsewhere.

The kind of doubt that followers of Jesus are able to experience is the kind that pushes us *into* Christ—the kind that leaves us asking questions but going back to Jesus, desperate for his help anyway. The kind that shuts our eyes to the circumstances in front of us to acknowledge our own deep belief in who the person of Christ is at his core.

But especially in seasons of hesitation, we must be diligent to hold on to the believing kind of doubt. The enemy would love nothing more than to lure us into unbelief, and this would be the perfect opportunity.

At the beginning of the book of James, the brother of Jesus begins his letter,

> Count it all joy, my brothers, when you meet trials of various kinds, for you know that the testing of your faith produces steadfastness. And let steadfastness have its full effect, that you may be perfect and complete, lacking in nothing. (James 1:2-4)

If I were the recipient of this letter, I'm not sure I would have kept reading.

BELIEF IN CHRIST DOES NOT GIVE US A PASS ON SUFFERING.

Nevertheless, his point was that belief in Christ does not give us a pass on suffering. In fact, those people who seem almost "entitled" to the most joy because they are the most righteous, might suffer the most affliction. And as much as that doesn't make sense to us in our "give me what I deserve" culture, it's the truth of Scripture.

Suffering happens regardless of our relationship with God.

James then follows up this thought that God works even in the suffering with this, "If any of you lacks wisdom, let him ask God, who gives generously to all without reproach, and it will be given to him. But let him ask in faith, with no doubting, for the one who doubts is like a wave of the sea that is driven and tossed by the wind." (James 1:5-6)

So, that would seem like it is NOT okay to doubt, right?

But the word used here for doubt is from the Greek word, diakrino, which means to "withdraw from."[1]

James tells us that when we ask God for something—for anything, including wisdom or discernment—we need to do it while pressing *in*, not pulling away.

Let me give you an example here.

All three of my kids have different personalities, strengths and weaknesses, fears and passions, just like all kids, which means they all have different opinions on roller coasters.

Last summer Jeff and I took them to Six Flags. Our youngest isn't quite tall enough to ride the biggest rides, but he wants to ride anything and everything he can get into. He might be unsure and a little scared, but he will still go. Every single time.

But our *oldest*? He is terrified of roller coasters, and he doesn't care who knows it. We can tell him up and down and sideways and back and forth that he absolutely will be okay if he rides the ride, that he will make it through. But he still sits out. Every single time.

That's the difference between believing doubt and unbelieving doubt. Believing doubt says, "God, I am unsure here. I don't see how you could possibly bring beauty out of these ashes. But I know who you are, and I know that you say you will, so I am going to walk forward and press in anyway. I will choose to believe, even though despite being unsure."

Unbelieving doubt says, "God, I am unsure here. I don't see how you could bring beauty out of these ashes. So I'm going to turn to someone or something else. I am going to try my best to make my own beauty. I am going to fill my pain with alcohol, drugs, sex, or Netflix."

Do you see the difference?

It's not the doubting itself that is the problem—it's whether the doubt presses you into Christ or pulls you away from him.

Take Eve, for instance.

I've always thought the original tactic of Satan was to question what God said. When we first meet the serpent in the garden, he finds Eve while she is alone and asks her "Did God actually say, 'You shall not eat of any tree in the garden?'" (Genesis 3:1)

This is so often how he starts with me, "Becky, did God *actually* say he loves you?"

And if you read the back and forth exchange, you'll see that Eve was certain on what God said. She replied to the serpent, "'We may eat of the fruit of the trees in the garden, but God said, 'You shall not eat of the fruit of the tree that is in the midst of the garden, neither shall you touch it, lest you die.'" (Genesis 3:3)

The serpent could have cut his losses for the day—his first tactic didn't work. Perhaps to his surprise, she *knew* what God commanded .

But the serpent, as we know, "was more crafty than any other beast"—just as he is today—and he didn't give up. So he changed his tactic from questioning *what* God said to *why* he said it. "But the serpent said to the woman, 'You will not surely die. For God knows that when you eat of it your eyes will be opened, and you will be like God, knowing good and evil.'" (Genesis 3:4)

He flat-out called God a liar. He convinced Eve into thinking that God was withholding something good from her. That he didn't have her best interest at heart, only his

THE ENEMY WANTS TO USE EVERY SITUATION THAT HE CAN TO PLANT DOUBT IN OUR HEARTS.

own. He tempted her to an unbelieving doubt. A doubt that caused her to pull away from God and trust herself instead. A doubt that caused her to sin.

The enemy wants to use every situation that he can to plant doubt in our hearts. We've seen it from the very beginning of time. But we must always remember that Satan uses our suffering as a temptation to pull us away while God uses it as an invitation to press in.

The Word of God is our greatest weapon against the enemy, but in order to use it, we have to *know* what it says. And often, even when we do our best to believe in the doubt, the enemy comes back to convince us of something different, just as he did to Eve. This is why we must be suited up with the armor of God at all times.

Paul writes in his letter to the Ephesians,

> Finally, be strong in the Lord and in strength of his might. Put on the whole armor of God, that you may be able to stand against the schemes of the devil. For we do not wrestle against flesh and blood, but against the rulers, against the authorities, against the cosmic powers over this present darkness, against the spiritual forces of evil in the heavenly places. (Ephesians 6:10-12)

Every time you wrestle with doubt, be on guard for the enemy to lure you away. Know what the Bible says about the character of God and your identity in Christ. Be prayerful, asking God to not only help you but refine you. Be in fellowship with other believers, allowing them to speak truth and grace in your life.

Qualify every doubt through the lens of Scripture, asking yourself whether it is pulling you to what you know about God or what you know about your circumstance. Do you have a believing or unbelieving kind of doubt? My hope is that you now know the difference and can move forward ready for any doubt that comes your way.

20 | AND STILL, WE WAIT

Doubt boils down to this: It can strengthen your relationship with Christ or weaken it. But be sre to keep this in mind, without doubt there wouldn't be faith. Hebrews 11 defines faith as "the assurance of things hoped for, the conviction of things not seen." (Hebrews 11:1)

Doubt will always be a part of our faith because until we meet Jesus face to face, our faith will not be made sight.

And so still, we wait.

We wait for God to come through. We wait for healing, for justice, for relational restoration. We wait for the diagnosis or the treatment. We wait for the job promotion or the career change. We wait for the earth to calm, for peace to be restored. We wait for our circumstances to get better or wait in fear for them to get worse. We wait for the next big

> **REALLY, WE'RE ALL JUST WAITING ON JESUS. AND OUR ONLY CHOICE HERE ON EARTH IS WHETHER WE WILL BELIEVE HIM IN THE MEANTIME.**

thing or the next hard thing.

But really, we're all just waiting on Jesus.

For Jesus to do what we want him to do, for him to show up and make us whole. We are waiting for something good to happen, something kind, some evidence of his faithfulness to enter back into our lives.

And we have to come to a point when we realize we will be waiting on that wholeness until we get to heaven. Our only choice here on earth is whether we will believe God in the meantime.

I've found that it comes more naturally to believe God when things are comfortable. I mean, this is probably an obvious observation, right? But believing God, even when it's harder, has always been worth it for me. And it will be for you too.

Believing God—even when I really, really, didn't want to—has never left me disappointed. He has always met me in my heartache. He has given me peace, hope, joy, and freedom. He has provided wisdom and discernment when I needed it most. He has surrounded me with people who love me. He hasn't changed my circumstances necessarily, but he has changed how I view them. . . and him.

That is what I so desperately hope for you, too.

I hope that you can now look back on your life and see how God has shown himself good, faithful, kind, or loving. I pray that you would now be able to write your own lessons of how God has shown up in your story just as I have. I hope that you could now be the one writing the chapters of this book, filled with miracles upon miracles, indicative of God's fervent presence in your own life.

And even as you wait, I pray that you are encouraged in your belief, in your doubt, and in everything between. God is clear about this: He loves you, and wants a relationship with you. Not only for all eternity, but in the here and now. He wants you to experience his abundance even while you're suffering and struggling to believe.

Jesus says, "The thief comes only to seal and kill and destroy. I came that [you] may have life and have it abundantly." (John 10:10) I hope you see how important you are to him today, right where you are. No matter your sin or your circumstance, I want you to believe this abundant life is yours today

I hope that you see my heart spilled across these pages is so you can see God's heart for you. These words are written so that you would find him worthy of your belief, like I have. That you would stop thinking God is for everyone else, and now know his promises for you, too, are good.

And ultimately, my prayer is that you would choose, over and over again, to believe it.

BUT YOU ARE A CHOSEN RACE, A ROYAL PRIESTHOOD, A HOLY NATION, A PEOPLE FOR HIS OWN POSSESSION, THAT YOU MAY PROCLAIM THE EXCELLENCIES OF HIM WHO CALLED YOU OUT OF DARKNESS INTO HIS MARVELOUS LIGHT.

1 peter 2:9

EPILOGUE

As previously mentioned, this has been a long process. Nearly two years ago I gave my forensic interview right before the entire world shut down with a global pandemic. It took a full year for our case to even go to the grand jury.

To give you more of the timeframe, in March of 2021, my father was indicted on three second degree felonies. Two weeks later he was arrested and one hour later he bonded out of jail. It is evident that he had a plan all along.

The next few months became a rollercoaster of lows and lower lows. Every time I thought, this can't get any worse, we found out something else.

He never confessed to his own family.

When asked about what happened to me, he would say, "You have to ask Becky."

When asked what happened in his marriage, he called it "an indiscretion."

When confronted with the possibility that there could be other people he harmed, he said, "Talk to my lawyer."

When offered a plea that took prison time off the table, his lawyer said, "He is no longer a threat and he'll take a polygraph to prove it."

When offered a plea that included sex offender registration, his lawyer said, "But, he'll likely lose his job."

And when it finally came down to the wire and a decision had to be made, he tried to weasel out of it once again.

I got the call while painting in my studio. The prosecutor said, "You're not going to like this, but I'm obligated to let you know what his lawyer said." I took a deep breath. "Your dad is willing to accept the sentence, but will only plead guilty to *one* felony count, not all three."

I tried not to throw the phone.

Even though the prosecutor explained this is a tactic often used by defense attorneys, I felt like my dad was calling me a liar. Like he was saying, "I'll agree so I can get on with it, but not because I did it."

I walked into the house and somehow made my way to Jeff's office. He quickly ended his conference call and I collapsed in his arms.

It was the most out of body experience I have ever had with grief.

My head was too heavy to hold up. My eyes were too swollen to open. My ears were ringing. The room was closing in on me. I slammed my hands down on the desk as he tried to figure out what was happening.

"He doesn't care! He doesn't care! He will never, ever, care!"

The *trauma* has never been the most traumatic part of this situation. It's all that has come after.

The thoughts of worthlessness. The feeling that I'll never measure up or be good enough. . . for my own father. I knew it all along, of course—his only concern was self-preservation. But this was the moment I finally understood it.

I hyperventilated in my counselor's office the next day.

Two days later, I got another call from the prosecutor we were

THE TRUTH IS, A GUILTY PLEA DOESN'T CHANGE ANYTHING FOR ME.

working with. "I can't believe I'm saying this. He will agree to everything. Three felony counts, ten years probation with deferred adjudication, and lifetime registration as a sex offender." Everything we were praying for.

I wish I could tell you I felt relieved. I wish I could tell you that I shouted for joy or felt victorious in that moment. But I didn't.

Instead, I crawled back into my bed with my heating pad and cup of hot tea and cried.

The truth is that a guilty plea doesn't change anything

for me.

My father still abused me.

He is still a sex offender, with or without registration.

He still doesn't care about me, or my siblings, or his family.

I am still hurt, heartbroken, and grieving.

And maybe you feel this way too.

Maybe, since you started this book, you have also received the answer to your prayer. Maybe you've witnessed the miracle you were hoping for. But maybe it hasn't changed how you feel or the circumstance that you're in either.

Your marriage staying together doesn't erase the infidelity.

Your adoption going through doesn't change your infertility.

Your amazing friend group doesn't change your singleness.

Your remission doesn't change your original diagnosis.

And, after all of our time spent together, I want to try and address this adequately.

God never promises happiness. He doesn't promise we will live on mountaintops instead of valleys. He doesn't tell us that once we walk on dry land in the middle of a sea, we'll never need a miracle again.

And he never says that one answered prayer will forever

fix our heartache.

And so now we pivot together once again.

We pivot back to the things we've learned about God in the waiting and suffering. We pivot back to the experiences we have had with him in the suffering. We pivot back to the lessons he has given us about truth, grace, love, and justice.

We pivot in the heartache, but we also pivot in the miracle. Because the miracle will never ultimately satisfy us. But Jesus will.

———————

Thursday, January 27, 2022 I woke up to a heart filled with peace. Today was the day to face my father in court. And I was ready.

A few days earlier, I screamed my head off at Jeff on the phone. It wasn't that I was angry with him in particular, he just happened to call at the wrong time. I cried and yelled, "What is wrong with me" while lying flat on the floor of my garage studio.

We prayed this day would come. . . I *wanted* this day to come. But as the time drew near, the doubt, anger, grief, and rejection began to creep back in.

I reminded myself, *But God will be with you.*

And on January 27th, Jeff and I walked into the courthouse. The rest of my family walked in shortly after. We rode the elevator up to the third floor together and met the prosecutor in the hallway. As he began to ask me some questions and explain the process to me, I got a glimpse of my dad coming out of the courtroom.

My fight-or-flight instinct kicked back in as I quickly moved out of his line of sight.

Cam, Lauren, Katie, and Trent had not seen or spoken to our father since March of 2018. My mom was in the same boat. And even though we all agreed to do what was in our own best interest, everyone showed up that day.

Seeing him in person is different than finding a picture hidden in the back of a drawer. Regardless of how prepared I was, watching him walk across a hallway quickened my heart rate.

I looked at the person who was speaking to me and shook my head, and backed away out of view while simultaneously moving my family in the same direction.

Tears threatened to fall and I reminded myself again, *But God is with you, Becky.*

The prosecutor asked to speak with Jeff and I for a moment. We walked back into the conference room, leaving our family in the cold and comfortless waiting room. He sat us down and explained the terms of probation that had been agreed to. Spoiler alert, probation is *not* getting off easy.

We asked a few questions and he reassured us that this was going to happen smoothly. *This part* was going to end today, after all this time. He looked at me with kindness in his eyes and said, "Becky, you are going to sleep better than you have in years tonight. Trust me." (He was right.)

We left his office and went back into the waiting room,

now filled with our not only our family but a growing tribe of people. Men and women who meant so much to us during this entire process showed up for the final day. They were here with us praying, encouraging, and supporting.

We gathered and hugged and before I knew it, it was time to go.

A DPS officer escorted us into the courtroom. We were the only case of the afternoon, and silently filed in one by one, filling up the entire left side. Our family sat on the front row, hand in hand in hand in hand. I leaned forward as the anxiety crept in, looked over at all of them and whispered, "I love you all so much."

Jeff gave me a sip of water as a touch of heartburn rose up inside of me. *But God is with you.*

Then my dad walked into the room and the air was suddenly different. Thick. Suffocating. Heavy.

He didn't make eye contact with anyone and didn't miss a step as he sat down, also on the front row, but opposite of us and on the very end.

Basically, he was as far away as he could possibly be. On purpose.

"All rise."

The judge walked in. Now, I want you to know that I am a crime-show junkie. I listen to all the podcasts and watch all the shows. But this was certainly not as glamorous as any episode of Law & Order that I had ever seen.

The judge quickly took his seat and quietly looked over papers for what seemed like forever. The room felt lopsided and under-lit. It was cold but stuffy, understated but overwhelming.

Finally, the judge said, "can both of the parties approach."

My dad stood and followed his attorney to the bench.

He folded his hands in front of him and stood with his legs shoulder-width apart. He swayed back and forth like he always had. His suit looked like it was three sizes too big. He wore a cloth mask over his nose and mouth. Maybe he was scared of covid, maybe he was trying to be respectful of the one other person in the room wearing a mask. But maybe, he was just trying to hide.

The judge asked him a series of questions making sure he understood the charges against him and the rights he was giving up by agreeing to a plea.

My dad quietly responded to each one with a simple, "Yes sir."

It looked like his legs just might give out from under him. My heart broke for him for just a moment, then I felt a thought rise up inside of me, *This is his consequence, not mine.*

The moment came when it was time for me to give a statement.

The ADA walked over to me, swung the gate open and led me to the witness chair. He whispered things like, "Take a breath. Take your time. We aren't in any hurry. This is your time to say what you need to say."

Even now I get emotional thinking about this moment

because I could have chosen differently. As much as we prayed for this day, this plea, and this sentence, it could have been done *apart* from us. I didn't have to be there—none of us did. We could have gotten the phone call and let it be what it was, never having to see him again.

But it was important to me from the very beginning to address him publicly in court.

So much of how he lived his life was *secret*. I wanted him to know that, once and for all, this would no longer be a secret. *Everyone* knew.

I sat in the chair, unfolded my piece of paper, and put my reading glasses on.

I took a deep breath.

And then maybe another.

"When given the opportunity to publicly address you, I felt overwhelmed with how to start."

I made a point to look up at him. I was about 15 feet from him and to my surprise I couldn't make out his face. Like, at all.

I moved my hand to pull my reading glasses off. I wanted to see him more clearly, but I sensed the Lord say, "No."

Another deep breath.

> "Should I tell you all the things I've held back for thirty years? Should I talk about the anxiety, depression, sleeplessness, and panic attacks we've since suffered? Should I speak for everyone you've hurt or just myself?

I eventually came to the conclusion that, in these few moments we have before us, I should tell you all the things I simply want you to know... as this will perhaps be the very last time I am able to speak with you.

First and foremost, I want to make something very clear: you are not the victim here today, I am. We are sitting here as a result of YOUR actions. Not mine.

Dad, You groomed me, molested me, and took advantage of my love for you. You manipulated me, you bribed me, you assaulted me. And even with all of that, I need you to know that I forgive you for the pain you've caused AND continue to cause our family.

I forgive you for lying to and about me. For being unfaithful to my mother, likely more times than I'll ever know. I forgive you for using me and manipulating me. I forgive you for being selfish, narcissistic and a liar. I forgive you for not protecting me even when you were supposed to be my fiercest protector.

For twenty years I gave you the benefit of the doubt. I loved you. I protected you. I fought for you. But as the abuse became more clear to me, so did your lies and manipulation. And the truth is the most traumatic part of this entire thing is knowing that my dad doesn't find me worth fighting for in return.

Two years ago we sat across from you at breakfast. I sobbed and hugged you. I told you repeatedly that I forgive you for the pain you have caused. I all but begged you to pursue a relationship with us while remaining very clear as to what boundaries I needed to draw. You said you were fine with that, and willing to do "anything" to make it right.

We haven't heard from you since that day.

For a long time I struggled with what that said about me. Maybe something is wrong with me. Maybe I'm just unloveable. Maybe I'm worthless. Maybe by setting firm boundaries I became useless to you.

And I've often wondered if it would be easier to hate you and not want the best for you. I've wondered if it would make the pain subside if I didn't care about you and your well being.

But I tried that and it doesn't work. The resentment and anger I felt for you took me to some of my darkest moments, making me cynical and bitter.

So It's important to me that you know THAT is why

I've chosen forgiveness. For MY sake, not yours. I've chosen it because it's the better road for me and my family, and because I know I need forgiveness too.

And despite everything you have said and not said, the things you have done and left undone, I truly want the best for you. I had originally hoped that THAT best would include relationships with your family - with us - but that time has now unfortunately come and gone.

My prayer for you moving forward is that the Holy Spirit would bring you to a place of true repentance and conviction. No amount of "I'm sorrys" or items crossed off a to do list can replace TRUE sorrow over your actions. You have to take ownership of the irreparable damage you have caused your family in order to move forward.

I pray that this day will not be the end but the beginning for you - the beginning of a life full of Hope that God can indeed bring beauty from these ashes for you. Perhaps now that you have this label attached to you you could finally stop PRETENDING this isn't your story too and start pursuing the true gospel - a gospel of GRACE, mercy, and restoration. And I pray now you will be forced to stop minimizing 10 years of child abuse as an "indiscretion."

Despite what it might seem, we are not here to publicly shame you but to protect other little girls from you. We never wanted your apologies but only to see and experience EVIDENCE of regret, remorse, and ultimately your unconditional love.

I will continue to trust that God will guide me to a place of healing, and ask that He show me the treasures brought only from this heartbreak. And I will trust Him to do the same for you. And I hope you'll let Him.

I made it through the entire statement without crying. But the second I was done, I grabbed that Kleenex on the table and darted out of the courtroom with the rest of our people.

I still can't get over what God did for me in those moments. Although my dad, and everyone else in the courtroom, thought I was making nearly constant eye contact with him, I have no knowledge of the expressions on his face.

I don't know if he was crying or smirking. I don't know if he nodded in agreement or shook his head in disbelief. I don't know if he scoffed at some of the things I said or shrugged his shoulders and brushed them off. I don't even know if he was paying attention.

God did not allow *one more* memory of him.

I didn't walk away feeling hopeful because I saw remorse. I didn't walk away angry because I saw resentment. I walked away confident that I had obeyed God.

Again, I wish this made it all feel better. But just as I anticipated, it didn't. I wish I could say that earthly justice makes it easier to move on, but again, it hasn't.

Although now, this chapter of my life feels closed. It feels like I can rest from constantly living on pins and needles, waiting for the next phone call or piece of news. And that *is* a relief— an answer to a prayer I never prayed. A miracle I never knew I needed, until it happened.

After all of this, and seeing it more clearly in the rear view mirror than when it was in front of me, I understand yet again that God really does work all things together. It's just that my idea of good and his idea are sometimes (maybe oftentimes) different.

But I'm learning to be okay with that.

Because I'm learning to believe it anyway. And now, you are learning to believe it too.

232   THE PIVOT

WITH GRATITUDE

This book has been a labor of love and in the works far before I'll ever know. Ten years ago, I wrote on my little family blog that I dreamt of writing a book some day. Never in my wildest dreams did I ever imagine that I would be spilling out my deepest, darkest, most shamed secret on the pages before you for the entire world to read.

But God.

He has been my rock and a redeemer through this entire process. God has been the first call and the last call on multiple occasions. And despite which one He ended up being in the moment, He never left. The thing I am most thankful for about Jesus is that he is faithful when I am faithless, and will continue to ever be.

To the Seven. This book is because of you. Thank you for believing me from day one. You have supported me, loved me, encouraged me, and believed with me.

Katie, thank you for showing up with Kleenex and a bottle of wine the very first night. Thank you for coming even though you had no earthly idea what you were walking into. Thank you for encouraging me to be brave and strong.

Trent, you will never know how much you mean to me. That very first night you said, "you are not alone in this now" and I will never ever forget that. Thank you.

Lauren, you are the calm for our family. You are strong and firm, but your presence is a relief for all of us, especially me. Thank you for speaking truth over me when I need it most.

Cam, you are the best brother we could ever ask for. From the very first moment I shared my secret with you, you rallied behind me. You fought for me, walked before me, and spoke for me when I couldn't speak for myself. You hugged me that first night and said, "you were made for this." Thank you for being you.

Mom, you are the strongest woman I have ever known. Your grace, poise, and strength has impacted everyone around you - especially the six of us. You have humbly led us toward forgiveness, peace, and righteousness throughout this entire process. I hope I never stop learning from you.

Julie and Craig, Thank you for being a safe place to land during all of this. Your prayers, tears, and belief from the very first words changed my story. You both never judged and always listened. I am ever grateful.

Sarah, thank you for being the inspiration for finishing the book, for believing God despite the most tragic of circumstances. I know that your belief will be counted to you as righteousness, just as it was to Abraham. Thank you for encouraging me to keep going even though I was hurting.

To our beloved Dan, I cannot wait to get one of your hugs when I get to heaven. Thank you for your encouragement as I wrote this book and walked this journey. I know you would have been one of the first ones to show up in my cheering section any day of the week. We love and miss you greatly.

Joanna, Thank you for reading anything and everything I've ever sent you. Thank you for loving me and believing in me from the very first minute we met. I am so glad we found our way back to each other.

Mary and Jen, thank you for inspiring me to finish and walk this road well. Thank you for praying for me and wiping my tears when it was difficult.

Chrissie and Lisa, thank you for pouring into me over the last 15 years. I wouldn't be who I am today without your influence on my life.

Medea, thank you for encouraging me to see a counselor. Ours is a friendship of divine intervention and I am forever grateful.

To Holly, I am so glad you moved back! Thank you for brainstorming with me, for dreaming with me, and for not letting me off the hook when I wanted to give up. You are a wonderful cheerleader.

To Terri, thank you for sharing your input and wisdom with me. This book wouldn't be what it is otherwise.

To Crystal, Emily, and Magen, Thank you for letting me know I could do this.

To Representative Goldman, aka, "The Other Craig," Thank you for going to bat for me, my family, and every other victim on the house floor. We all love you so much. . . *especially* our kids.

To Mikaela, thank you for literally making sure all of my i's were dotted and t's were crossed. This book wouldn't be what it is without you.

Brady, Charlotte, and Landry: Being your mom is the privilege of a lifetime. Thank you putting up with me learning these lessons and applying them to my life. Thank you for enduring the long nights, the short tempers, and the extraneous tears that undoubtedly affected you during this period of life.

My prayer is that you would always see God through my brokenness and be encouraged to believe him when you encounter your own heartache. I hope that when you are able to fully understand your family's story, you would not see the ashes that resulted, but the beauty that came from God's love covering it all.

To my very best friend and the love of my life. My champion, my warrior, my fiercest advocate, Jeff Leach. There are literally no words in the English language to describe my gratitude for the ways you have supported me over the last twenty five years. I know you would change it if you could. I know you would take my pain if you could. I know you would walk the road for me if you could. But thank you for being by my side as I did it for myself.

Thank you for holding me as my nightmares subsided.

Thank you for fighting for my voice to be heard. Thank you for making it possible for me to be a wife, mom, sister, and friend while walking through the darkest season of my life. Thank you for being patient, gracious, loving, and kind as I navigated the depths of my unbelief. But most of all, thank you for believing God when I couldn't and reminding me to do it anyway. I will be eternally grateful that you are by my side. I love you as far as the ends of the earth reach.

And finally, to every woman who has bought, loved, read, and re-read this book : these words were written for you. Thank you for letting these lessons be a part of your journey too. These pages have been prayed over, cried over, and poured over in an effort to give you the very best of myself. My prayer for you is to believe God deeper and stronger as a result of this outpouring. That you would stand convinced of his love for you, his strength inside of you, and his wisdom before you.

Now, let's go pivot.

NOTES

Chapter 1, *It Starts With a Thing*

1. "peripateō." Interlinear Bible Search. 2 Corinthians 5 :7. https://www.studylight.org/study-desk/interlinear.html?q1=2%20corinthians+5:7. Accessed February 8, 2022.

Chapter 4, *The Pivot*

1. "pivot." Merriam-Webster.com Dictionary, Merriam-Webster, https://www.merriam-webster.com/dictionary/pivot. Accessed February 7, 2022.

Chapter 5, *Choosing Joy or Choosing Belief*

1. "ménō." Interlinear Bible Search. John 15:5. https://www.studylight.org/lexicons/eng/greek/3306.html. Accessed February 7, 2022.

Chapter 8, *Believing God's Purposes are Good*

1. Britannica, The Editors of Encyclopaedia. "Chemosh". Encyclopedia Britannica, 10 Sep. 2007, https://www.britannica.com/topic/Chemosh. Accessed February 9, 2022.

Chapter 9, *Believing God is Your Strength*

1. Henry, Matthew. Concise Commentary on Exodus 17. Matthew Henry Concise Commentary on the Whole Bible. 1706. https://www.studylight.org/commentaries/eng/mhn/exodus-17.html Accessed February 8, 2022.

Chapter 13, *Believing God will Redeem*

1. "Redeem." Merriam-Webster.com Dictionary, Merriam-Webster, https://www.merriam-webster.com/dictionary/redeem. Accessed February 7, 2022.

2. "Reconcile." Merriam-Webster.com Dictionary, Merriam-Webster, https://www.merriam-webster.com/dictionary/reconcile. Accessed February 7, 2022.

Chapter 14, *Believing God Chose You*

1. "Rejected." Dictionary.com, https://www.dictionary.com/browse/rejected. Accessed February 10, 2002.

Chapter 16, Believing God is Just

1. Henry, Matthew. Complete Commentary on Romans 12. Henry's Complete Commentary on the Whole Bible. 1706. https://www.studylight.org/commentaries/eng/mhm/romans-12.html. Accessed February 8, 2022.

Chapter 18, *When We Doubt*

1. Blackaby, Henry T, Richard Blackaby, and Claude V. King. Experiencing God: Knowing and Doing the Will of God. Nashville, Tenn: Broadman & Holman

Publishers, 2008.

Chapter 19, *Believing Doubt vs. Unbelieving Doubt*

1. "Diakrínō." Interlinear bible search: James 1:5-6. https://www.studylight.org/study-desk/interlinear.html?q1=James+1:6. Accessed February 9, 2022.

ABOUT THE AUTHOR

Becky is a fervent writer, accidental speaker & self-taught artist. She adores instagram, hates working out and is obsessive over the creamer in her coffee. She is a mom of three and married to her high school sweetheart, who just so happens to also be her State Representative. The beat of Becky's heart is to equip women to live free in the grace of Jesus's steadfast love.

The Pivot is Becky's first book. Scan the QR Code below to get instant access to Becky's website, instagram page, interviews, and her art shop. Becky also puts out a weekly email called, "The Leach Letter" that offers encouragement, inspiration, and hope to all of her subscribers.

Made in the USA
Las Vegas, NV
05 May 2024

89574508R00144